W9-APN-608

HUMAN ACTS

HUMAN ACTS

An Essay in their Moral Evaluation

BY

ERIC D'ARCY

LECTURER IN PHILOSOPHY IN THE
UNIVERSITY OF MELBOURNE

BJ1012
D21h

64818

ST. JOSEPH'S UNIVERSITY	STX

BJ1012.D21h

Human acts;

3 9353 00002 5625

OXFORD
AT THE CLARENDON PRESS
1963

Oxford University Press, Amen House, London E.C.4

GLASGOW NEW YORK TORONTO MELBOURNE WELLINGTON
BOMBAY CALCUTTA MADRAS KARACHI LAHORE DACCA
CAPE TOWN SALISBURY NAIROBI IBADAN ACCRA
KUALA LUMPUR HONG KONG

© *Oxford University Press 1963*

PRINTED IN GREAT BRITAIN

PREFACE

I wish to acknowledge my great indebtedness to Professor H. L. A. Hart. He helped me at every stage in the writing of this book, read the manuscript, and saved me from many mistakes and inelegancies. I am particularly grateful, too, to Miss G. E. M. Anscombe and Professor Gilbert Ryle for many illuminating and profitable discussions. My thanks are also due to Professor A. Boyce Gibson, Mrs. P. R. Foot, and Mr. J. M. Hinton for a number of valuable suggestions.

E. D'A.

CONTENTS

PART II. MOTIVES

INTRODUCTION

FOR many years philosophers have studied two aspects of the problem of Moral Evaluation: first, the meaning, function, and mutual relationship of the *predicates* of moral evaluation—e.g. good and bad, right and wrong; and second, the *logical classification* of the propositions in which they are expressed. This book is concerned with a third aspect of the problem: the *subject* of these propositions—the human act or performance itself. Very little work has been done on this since Bentham. A great deal has indeed been written on the topic of Acts, but this has been mainly from the point of view of philosophical psychology and the logical grammar of act-terms and act-propositions. My own purpose, however, is to examine the human act from the standpoint of ethics: to ask, What is the relevance of the several elements of an act to its characterization in moral discourse, and to its moral evaluation?

Hume contended in the *Treatise*, and again in the *Enquiry*, that an *action* can never be the object of moral approval or disapproval; only the agent's motive, or his character, can be the object of moral appraisal; an act is relevant to such appraisal only in so far as it is a symptom of a certain quality of mind. Reid took Hume to task for this in his fifth *Essay on the Active Powers*, though only briefly. It was left to Bentham to make a thorough examination of those aspects of an act which must be considered in passing judgement upon it, in his *Principles of Morals and Legislation*. He studied them carefully through seven chapters, which occupy one hundred and seven pages in the Clarendon Press edition. I propose to pursue some of the points which he raised there.

At the beginning of his inquiry, after showing why he

believes that similar rules provide the grounds for moral and legal censure, Bentham writes:

In every transaction which is examined with a view to punishment, there are four articles to be considered: 1. The *act* itself, which is done. 2. The *circumstances* in which it is done. 3. The *intentionality* that may have accompanied it. 4. The *consciousness*, unconsciousness, or false consciousness, that may have accompanied it. . . . There are also two other articles on which the general tendency of an act depends: and on that, as well as on other accounts, the demand which it creates for punishment. These are, 1. The particular *motive* or motives which gave birth to it. 2. The general *disposition* which it indicates.[1]

This suggests a plan for my own essay. I shall not consider the question of disposition, but I shall take up the other five 'articles'. Since Bentham frequently calls intentionality and consciousness 'circumstances', the first four articles will be dealt with under the title, 'Act and Circumstances', in Part I; and the fifth article will be considered in Part II, 'Motives'.

In this essay, then, I am not attempting to address myself to the whole range of questions which suggest themselves as relevant to the examination of an act with a view to its moral evaluation, but only to some of those which are suggested by Bentham's account. However, this is not an essay on Bentham, nor on this particular book of Bentham; some of the questions he raises, and some of the criticisms which his answers seem to invite, serve simply as so many points of departure for investigation. Furthermore, although I venture to put forward a number of conclusions different from Bentham's, I do not here propose any general ethical doctrine in place of his Utilitarianism. His argument is guided and controlled throughout, sometimes with an astonishing consistency, by his

---

[1] *Introduction to the Principles of Morals and Legislation* (Oxford, 1907), pp. 71–72. All subsequent references to Bentham relate to this book, unless otherwise noted.

Principle of Utility, but it frequently leads him to conclusions which are at odds with ordinary language. My own aim is rather to look for some of the assumptions about acts, and some of the rules for their moral evluation, which are present or implicit in our day-to-day discussions and appraisals of human action and behaviour.

PART I
ACT AND CIRCUMSTANCES

1

ACT, CONSEQUENCES, AND CIRCUMSTANCES

'In some circumstances', says Bentham, 'even to kill a man may be a beneficial act; in others, to set food before him may be a pernicious one.' The point is well taken. Asked whether one believes that it is wrong to do X, one often has to say that it depends on the circumstances; in some circumstances it would be wrong, in others it may be permissible, or even commendable; circumstances alter cases. But there is a prior point. Circumstances may affect not only one's final moral evaluation of an act, but also one's characterization of it: in some circumstances X is P, in others it is Q. In performing 'the very same act', one is tempted to say, a person may, in different circumstances, be doing different things: in signing his name, for example, he may be drawing a cheque, entering a contract, or giving his autograph to an admirer. Indeed, he may even be doing opposite things: issuing a death-warrant, or granting a reprieve.

In examining an act with a view to its moral evaluation, then, we must study the role of Circumstances, and the way that 'act' and 'circumstances' are mutually related in the composition of a good or bad deed. Bentham does so in terms of their consequences; but he does not tell us what he means by 'act', nor how it is to be distinguished from 'consequences'. I shall begin, therefore, by investigating that distinction.

§ 1. ACT AND CONSEQUENCES

The question with which our inquiry begins is this: In analysing the elements which constitute a given human performance, how are we to decide which of them belong to the act and which of them belong to the consequences of the act? We may illustrate the point at issue with two examples. First, A tells a lie and B is deceived; A is thus able to rob B. Where are we to draw the line between 'act' and 'consequences'? Are we to say that A's *act* is simply 'deceiving B', with the *consequence* of being in a position to rob him? Or is A's act 'telling a lie', with the two consequences (1) B is deceived, and (2) A is thus in a position to rob him? Second, Macbeth killed Duncan, and as a consequence of that act became King. But could one not also say that Macbeth stabbed Duncan, and as a consequence of this act the King died? Was his *act* 'stabbing', which produced the *consequence* of the King's death; the further consequence of Macbeth's becoming King following from the circumstances of Duncan's being King and Macbeth's standing in (some sort of) line to the throne? Or was his act 'killing the King', with the consequence of succeeding to the throne? The examples indicate one possible answer to our question. Perhaps the line to be drawn between 'act' and 'consequences' is not a fixed line: perhaps it is possible to make several different but equally correct statements as to what is the act and what the consequences. Let us first consider two other answers that stand at opposite extremes.

(i) *Two extremes*

During the racial troubles in Arkansas in 1956, Professor J. J. C. Smart read a paper in defence of Extreme Utilitarianism. In the discussion which followed, he considered a hypothetical case in which white people believed that some crime had been committed by a negro. Since the criminal's identity was not established they proposed to lynch five negroes chosen at random. The local sheriff knew this, and after investigation felt that the only alternative was to arrest some negro, 'frame' a case against him, 'pack' the jury, and have him found guilty, sentenced to death, and shot. From premises of Extreme Utilitarianism Smart argued that, if this were indeed the only alternative to the lynching of the five, he would be a wicked man if he did not carry out the plan; and that the correct description of what he did would be, not 'judicial murder', but 'saving four lives.'[1] There are, of course, two separate problems here: one, Was the sheriff justified, or even obliged, so to act? the other, What would be the correct characterization of such an act? It is only with the latter that we are concerned.

Now suppose that the sheriff himself acted as executioner; consider the following possible descriptions of his last act in the drama:

1. He tensed his forefinger.
2. He pressed a piece of metal.
3. He released a spring.
4. He pulled the trigger of a gun.
5. He fired a gun.
6. He fired a bullet.
7. He shot a bullet at a man.
8. He shot a bullet towards a man.
9. He shot a man.
10. He killed a man.
11. He committed judicial murder.
12. He saved four lives.

One possibility would be to say that the sheriff's act was to tense his finger, with the consequence that he pressed a piece of metal; another, that his act was to press a piece of metal,

[1] This was put forward purely for the sake of discussion, to see where such a suggestion might lead. I do not wish to imply, here or elsewhere, that Professor Smart personally holds this view.

with the consequence that he released a spring; another, that his act was to kill a man, with the consequence that he saved five others; or simply, that his act was to save four lives. At one extreme, then, is Smart's suggestion that the last is the correct characterization.

At the opposite extreme is the theory of the nineteenth-century jurist Austin, which has passed into a good deal of modern legal theory, and with some modification into more purely philosophic writing: for instance, in Prichard. The following remarks are taken from the eighteenth of Austin's Lectures in Jurisprudence:

Certain movements of our bodies follow invariably and *immediately* our wishes and desires for these *same* movements. . . . If my arm be free from disease, and from chains and other hindrances, my arm rises, so soon as I wish that it should. . . . These antecedent wishes and these consequent movements are human *volitions* and *acts* (strictly and properly so called). They are the only objects to which those terms properly apply. . . . The wishes which are immediately followed by the bodily movements wished, are the only wishes *immediately followed by their objects* . . . the only wishes which attain their *ends* without the intervention of *means*. In every other instance of wish or desire, the object of the will is attained (in case it be attained) through a *series* of means: each of the means being (in its turn) the object of a distinct wish; and each of them being wished (in its turn) as a step to that object which is the end at which we aim. . . . And as our desires of those bodily movements which immediately follow our desires for them are the only *volitions*; so are the bodily movements, by which they are immediately followed, the only *acts* or *actions* (properly so called). . . . As the bodily movements which immediately follow volitions are the only *ends* of volition, it follows that those bodily movements are the only objects to which the term 'acts' can be applied with perfect precision and propriety. . . . Most of the names which seem to be names of acts are names of acts *coupled with certain of their consequences*. For example, if I kill you with a pistol or gun I *shoot* you. And the long train of incidents which are denoted by that brief expression are considered (or spoken of) as if they constituted an act perpetrated by me. In truth the only parts of the train which are my act or acts are the muscular motions by which I raise the weapon, point it at your head or body, and pull the trigger. These I *will*. The contact of the flint and steel; the ignition of the powder, the flight of the ball towards your body, the wound and subsequent death, with the numberless incidents included in these are *consequences* of the act which I *will*. I *will* not those consequences, though I may intend them.[1]

This offers a clear answer to our question; for Austin, the line between 'act' and 'consequences' is to be drawn at the point where muscular control ends. The term 'act' applies only to voluntary movements of the limbs, organs, or muscles; the term 'circumstances' to any relevant facts prior to or con- comitant with the act; and the term 'consequences' to the events subsequent to, and caused by, that act in those circum- stances. For Austin, then, the sheriff's *act* would be tensing his forefinger; the *circumstances* of the act, that his finger was on the trigger of a cocked and loaded gun which was pointing at a man whom he had framed; the *consequences* of his act, the movement of the trigger, the release of the hammer, the ex- plosion of the cartridge, the expulsion of the bullet, its flight towards the victim, its entry into his body, his wound and death; plus, of course, whatever followed from that. In the litany, suggested above, of twelve possible answers to the question, 'What was his act?', Austin would say that only the first is correct. Notice that it is not the fourth, 'He pulled the trigger', but 'the muscular motions by which' he pulled the trigger; hence, 'He tensed his forefinger'.

The argument that leads to this conclusion seems to take four steps. First, only a voluntary act is an act; second, only that which is immediately produced by the will is voluntary; third, only the movements of certain muscles, organs, and limbs can be immediately produced by the will; therefore, fourth, only those movements can be acts. Each of these

[1] *Lectures in Jurisprudence* (London, 1885), vol. i, pp. 411–15.

steps presents difficulties. For instance, the first suggests that the phrase 'voluntary act' is pleonastic, and the phrase 'involuntary act' self-contradictory. But this is to deal rather high-handedly with English usage. If the act X is ascribed to A, it makes perfectly good sense to accept the ascription as correct, but to inquire whether or not the act was voluntary; whereas if murder is ascribed to him, it does not make sense to accept the ascription as correct and to inquire whether or not his victim died. If A is accused of having done X, and one pleads on his behalf that X was 'not a voluntary act', it is the adjective that one is stressing, not the noun: one is saying that, though admittedly A did in some sense do X, he did not do it in the relevant sense, viz. 'voluntarily'. If it were the noun which one meant to stress, one would not say, 'X was not a voluntary act', but something quite different: for instance, '*A* did not do X; *B* did'.

It is curious that Austin is apparently satisfied to treat *act* and *action* as synonymous. He is right, of course, in suggesting that there are many bodily movements which are not 'acts'. We may think of the beating of the heart, the circulation of the blood, the functioning of the liver, motions within the brain, the expansion and contraction of the pupil of the eye, the imperceptible growth of the finger-nails and hair, the working of the salivary glands; it is quite true that these phenomena are not called 'acts'; but on Austin's theory they would also lose the name of 'action'. That would be odd; for we often speak of the action of the heart, the action of the salivary glands, the action of the liver, and so on; and these actions are not called acts. When may we substitute 'act' for 'action'? As a general rule, an action is called an act only when it can be described in a proposition with a personal subject; the actions of signing a cheque or killing a rival are acts, for one can say, 'I signed the cheque', or 'He killed his rival'; but the beating of the heart and the working of the liver are not acts: one cannot say, 'I beat my heart', or 'I worked my liver'. The fact that one may say, 'I am bleeding', does not tell against this test, for the test applies only to *actions* which may be called acts; and one does not naturally call bleeding an action. Wittgenstein contrasts things that simply *happen* to us, such as the subsidence of a violent thudding of the heart, with things that we *do*, such as raising an arm. If one were asked, 'What were you doing at noon yesterday?', the answer, 'Bleeding from the nose', would be taken for a slightly grim form of humour; and the humour arises from the fact that bleeding is not something that one 'does': it is not an action, let alone an act. A slightly different version of the test is to say that one may substitute 'act' for 'action' only when the action may be spoken of as 'my action': for example, the action of signing a cheque, or killing a man, may be called 'my action', and is an act; the beating of the heart cannot be called 'my action', and is not an act. It is true that a doctor discussing a patient may speak of 'his heart-action': but this is probably medical shorthand for 'his heart's action', and, as Wittgenstein would say, the heart-action is not something that one does.

Every act, then (whether voluntary or involuntary), is an action; but not every action is an act. The sense of the term 'action' which applies to bodily movements which are not acts is rather akin to the sense of the term 'action' in which it is used in the language of processes: of the language, for instance, of chemical processes, as 'the action of sulphuric acid on iron filings', 'the action of light on a photographic plate', 'the action of the gastric juices on the food in the stomach'; or the language of physical processes, as 'the action of the sea on the rocks'; or the language of mechanical processes, as 'the action of the cylinders in a V8-type engine', 'the action of the wheels in a pulley'. In none of these cases does one naturally substitute 'act' for 'action'; and the word 'process' provides a rough criterion for distinguishing between those events taking place in or proceeding from us which are involuntary acts, and those which are not. The term 'involuntary acts' does not apply to those events which either simply are, or are closely analogous to, chemical, physical, or mechanical processes which could take place in a non-human system or apparatus; it does often apply to those events which are similar to actions which I perform voluntarily. The action of the heart is not an act, either voluntary or involuntary: in neither sense is it something one 'does'; the action of overturning a bottle of ink on one's desk is an act, which may be voluntary or involuntary: one may 'do' it in either sense. Other types of involuntary act, or action, may be voluntarily inhibited or imitated; but process-type actions cannot. One may delay a sneeze; a trained actor may mimic a nervous twitch, or sneeze at will; but one cannot at will, unfortunately, affect the functioning of the liver. One may imitate the action of the tiger; but one cannot have one's heart imitate the action of the tiger's heart.

Austin's theory carries the further implication that only a physiologist could tell us the name of our acts. When I speak, for instance, my *act*, what I *do*, is not 'to speak', but to tighten certain muscles in and around and behind my mouth; the sounds produced are simply *consequences* of my act. I could not name or identify the muscles involved, and am not aware of the existence of most of them; yet on this theory it is my desire for their movement which causes them to move. There is irony in this. One defect of a theory such as Austin's, as we shall see in Chapter 3, is its inability to account for the fact that people are often held responsible for actions which were not preceded by conscious choice or 'act of the will', e.g. omissions through negligent inadvertence; yet the theory involves the conclusion that one is hardly ever conscious of the main elements of one's voluntary act, viz. the muscles which one moves by one's desire for their movement, though usually not knowing of their existence. To find out what I 'really do' I should have to consult a trained physiologist. Only he could tell me, too, with a precision and a certainty that the most skilful psychoanalyst might well envy, what I 'really desire'—when I speak, or open a door, or press the self-starter button of my car: for he alone knows the muscular contractions which on Austin's theory are caused by my desire for them, and constitute my act.

The theory therefore offers answers to two questions: (1) To what does the term 'act' apply? (2) What is it for an act to be voluntary? The answer to the second has much in common with the theories of Hume and Thomas Brown, as well as of Prichard. This kind of answer has been attacked, successfully as it seems to me, by Wittgenstein, Ryle, and Hart. But even were one to grant Austin his answer to the second question, his answer to the first would not be thereby established. It involves dealing high-handedly with other phrases in ordinary language than 'involuntary acts'. For moral discourse it carries the implication that no act can be morally good or bad, right or wrong; no act-term can be the subject of a proposition expressing a moral evaluation; murder, treason, and rape are not bad or wicked acts, because they are not acts: they are acts followed by many, complex, consequences. But Austin's doctrine goes wider even than that. It boldly proclaims that most of the names which we speak of as denoting acts do not do so at all: to kick or punch, to lift or carry, to speak, or strike a match, or sign a contract—none of these is an act. But surely a particular theory about the will warrants no such conclusions about the language of acts. There is no parallel here with a scientist who, after careful experimental research, announces that, contrary to prevailing opinion, X is not really A: say, that smallpox is not a virus-disease, or that a certain metal is not an element. There is a standard definition of A—of what a virus-disease is, or an element—and he reports his finding that, in the case of X, some element of the definition is not verified. But Austin is not taking the standard definition of 'act' and showing that some element of it is lacking in the things which we usually call acts; he is, in effect, telling us that the standard definition is wrong: that what the word is thought to mean, both in ordinary and philosophical usage, is not what it *really* means.

(ii) *Three theses*

As answers to our question, then, Smart's suggestion and Austin's theory stand at opposite extremes. In suggesting that the truth lies somewhere between them, I shall put forward three theses. The first is of rather general application; the second and third apply specifically to the problem of distinguishing between 'act' and 'consequence'.

Thesis One: There is not necessarily one, and only one, correct description of a given act. This tells against the implication of a theory such as Austin's, that it is only a trained physiologist who can give the correct description of an act; and it helps to reassure us about the connotation and denotation of the term 'act' in ordinary language. Three points may be made.

1. The description of an act appropriate to a given occasion may vary with the specialized interest of the inquirer or narrator. In the list, given above, of twelve contemplated alternative descriptions of a given episode, there is none that can be rejected as simply false, but the first eight would in most contexts, and certainly in contexts where a moral evaluation or legal trial of the act was being made, be misleading in various degrees. Justice would not be done if, in a subsequent trial, the sheriff were exonerated because 'All he did was to release a spring'.

But there are contexts in which the first of those twelve descriptions ('He tensed his forefinger'), or the third ('He released a spring'), could be the most appropriate answer to the question 'What did he do?' because of the special sort of answer required by the questioner, the particular aspect of the incident in which he was interested. For instance, a person who is being introduced to fire-arms for the first time, and learning to shoot, may have got as far as loading and cocking the gun, holding and aiming it, and crooking his right fore-finger on the trigger. Later he happens to be watching a news-reel film of the execution, and sees the sheriff carry out the movements which he himself has learnt; then there is a re-port, and the negro falls; and he asks, 'What did the sheriff do after he got his hands and fingers right?' The answer, 'He tensed, or suddenly squeezed, his forefinger', would then be perfectly in place. Again, a student of elementary ballistics may know that the bullet is driven out of the barrel by the gases which are suddenly released when the cartridge ex-plodes, and that the cartridge is exploded by the sudden impact of the hammer upon it; but why did the hammer make such an impact when the sheriff pulled the trigger? The answer will begin with an explanation of the way that trigger and hammer are connected by a spring-mechanism, and conclude with some such words as, 'So you see, when he pulled the trigger he released the spring.'

The same is true of some interests of an observer or in-quirer a little less highly specialized. For instance, a spectator of a game of poker might say, 'A is relaxing while waiting his turn to bid'; but a player who has made a close study of the mannerisms of each member of his school may say (to him-self), 'A is closing his eyes and leaning sideways in his chair; that means that he's going to bluff.' Or to take a different sort of case, think of a clerk still at his desk two hours after the time that the office usually closes. To the question, 'What are you doing?', he may give different answers to different in-quirers. For instance, to his wife on the telephone he may say, 'I'm working late'; to the manager of the firm, 'I'm finishing the Blair contract at the request of the Department Head'; to the Department Head, 'I'm just beginning the last clause'; to a policeman who has noticed a light burning unusually late, 'It's quite all right, Officer, I work here'; to a trade union official, 'It's all right, I'm getting double rates for working overtime'. Each of these different answers may be perfectly true and, according to the particular concern of each questioner, perfectly appropriate.

2. A different factor is the presence of specialized efforts, interests, or intentions of the agent. Hart has pointed out that there are occasions when my act, what I intend to do, is precisely to produce a particular muscular contraction: as, for example, when, in a gymnasium, the instructor says, 'Lift your right hand and contract the muscles of the upper arm.' Hampshire has remarked that, although at a given moment there may be a set of possible true answers to the question 'What are you doing now?', there is generally one that seems to the agent peculiarly appropriate to his present intentions. We might think of a test-pilot who could truthfully answer, 'Holding the joy-stick'; 'Looking through the windscreen'; 'Listening to the control-tower'; 'Smoking a cigarette'; or, 'Flying over the North Sea'. But the answer that seemed most appropriate to him might be, 'Testing the new Vickers jet.' Probably it was in these last terms that he would look forward to 'what he would be doing' on this day, or apologize for being unable to accept some other commitment; and if he were later trying to 'date' some other event, he might say, 'It must have been Tuesday, because I remember it was the day before I was to test the new Vickers jet.'

The agent's intention may have a very different effect. Instead of rendering one of several possible true descriptions of a given overt act more or less *appropriate* than another description, it may make the difference between a particular description's being *true or false*. Several people, A, B, and C, may be performing the same overt act; yet because of their different intentions, it may be true to say that A is doing X, B is doing Y, and C is doing Z: though false to say that A is doing Y or Z, B doing X or Z, or C doing X or Y. For instance, in the Deep South of the United States there are some 'All White' restaurants, and coloured people have sometimes recently made a point of entering them and eating there. A white man who sat and ate beside them might describe his action as joining their protest; or, perhaps making a slightly different point, as showing his solidarity with all citizens of the U.S.A.; or, quite differently, as simply having his lunch, 'not being interested in politics'; or, quite differently again, as reporting the incident for his newspaper. The point holds for acts of omission as well as for positive acts. For example, think of four people who, over a significant period of time, are abstaining from food. It may be that four quite different descriptions characterize their action, or omission: one of them is dieting, or slimming; another, hunger-striking; the third, keeping a religious fast; the other, conducting experiments on the nutritional needs of the human body. Within each of these descriptions, other descriptions, more precise and mutually exclusive, are possible: the third person, for instance, may be fasting to observe the Mohammedan Ramadan or the Christian Lent; and if the latter, it may be an act of impetration on behalf of a friend, or an act of atonement on behalf of a friend, or an act of atonement for his own sins, or a step in a deliberately plotted ascetic programme, say, in the 'Purgative Way'. It may then be that, according to the person's intentions, several of these descriptions would be not only inappropriate, but false. This is so because some of these act-descriptions are verbs which are defined in terms of intention; one may intend, or not intend, to do them; but one cannot do them unintentionally. The definitions of these verbs include, as a common element, the same physical movement or non-movement, but the specifying element is the particular intention; hence according to the different intentions, different verbs will be required. If the verbs X, Y, and Z are defined respectively as pr, ps, and pt, where p is the overt action common to all three, and r, s, and t the several proper intentions: then according to the presence of r, s, or *t*, the act will be described as X, Y, or Z. There will commonly be a general term for *p*, which will therefore be truly applicable to each of the three people who are performing the different acts X, Y, and Z; though of course it will be less informative. Thus the description, 'keeping Ramadan', applies only to the Moslem: it conveys the fact that he is fasting, and a number of other facts as well; but the general description, 'fasting', could be applied either to the Moslem or the Christian: and to the Christian bent on impetration, personal or vicarious atonement, or personal spiritual progress.

3. A third point draws attention to the fact that makes the other two possible. One's description of a person's act may vary according to the special interest of the inquirer or the specialized intention of the agent because, as Hampshire says, at any moment of a man's waking life there is always a set of possible true answers to the question, 'What is he doing now?' All the following answers to that question might be true at the very same time of, say, an actor who is in his dressing-room in a theatre: 'Sitting in a chair'; 'Warming himself in front of the fire'; 'Breathing quickly'; 'Resting his sore ankle'; 'Holding a book in his left hand'; 'Tapping his right hand on the arm of his chair'; 'Moving his eyes backwards and forwards'; 'Reading'; 'Reading *The Cherry Orchard*'; 'Memorizing his part'; 'Waiting to be called on stage for rehearsal'; 'Fulfilling a contract'. Clearly the possibilities of multiple alternative descriptions are very numerous; it would be difficult even to summarize the main headings of cases in which one may equally well say of a person either that he is doing X, or that he is doing Y. For instance, (1) X may be a species of the genus Y: as one may say of a surgeon that he is amputating a limb, or performing an operation; or of a woman, that she is making the beds, or doing housework. (2) X may be a tactic in the strategy Y: as one may say of a general that he is bringing up a unit into a new position, or strengthening his left flank; or of a politician, that he is

advocating more liberal terms for marriage-loans, or building up support among the younger voters. (3) X may be one of several possible ways of doing Y: as one may say of a mother, that she is reading to the children, or putting them to sleep; or of a golfer, that he is exploding out of a bunker, or playing out of it. (4) X may be a step in the process Y, or a part of the operation Y: as one may say of a surgeon that he is making an incision, or performing an operation; or of a chef, that he is turning a joint, or cooking a meal. (5) X may be a particular duty or function of the station in life or official position Y: as one may say of a judge, that he is hearing a case, or administering justice; or of a viceroy, that he is opening Parliament, or governing a colony. (6) Y may be a consequence, and especially an intended consequence, of the act X. This is the case with which we are concerned, and it brings us to our second thesis. Our first thesis has been concerned with act-descriptions in general; our second applies specifically to 'act' and 'consequences'.

Thesis Two: The term which denotes the act, in the description of a given incident, may often be elided into the term which denotes a consequence of the act: 'doing X with the consequence Y', may often be re-described simply as 'doing Y'. For instance, if A stabbed B, and thus killed him, we may say simply that A killed B. The act of flicking a switch may produce the consequences that (1) contact is made between two points, so that (2) current flows from outside the room, through these points and the wire in the room, into the globe and through its filament, and thus (3) the globe is illuminated; but this may also be described simply as, 'putting on the light', or 'lighting the lamp'. If a person sings a song, and thus entertains a group of people, we may say either that he is singing a song, or entertaining them; and if as a result of the latter he raises money for the Red Cross, we may say that he is raising money for the Red Cross; and if as a result of that he boosts morale, or helps the war effort, we may also say that he is boosting morale, or helping the war effort. We may therefore often *elide* one possible description, the term X, into another term Y, where (1) Y is the result or consequence of the agent A's doing X; (2) A is nevertheless said to be doing Y, e.g. entertaining people; (3) the elision is so complete that Y gives no hint of the specific nature of X.

As a rule, then, the line between 'act' and 'consequence' may be drawn at different points when the elements of a given episode are being analysed. If a is the number of relevant elements comprised in the term which is used to denote the act, c the number of relevant elements comprised in the term used to denote the consequences, and t the number of relevant elements comprised in the description of the whole episode, so that

$$a = t - c:$$

then while t is of course a constant for a given episode, a and c are variables. But now, is this true for all values of a and c, or is their range of possible values restricted? In answer to this question I shall make three suggestions, of which the first two simply state in different form conclusions already reached.

First, apart from special contexts of the sort we have noticed, there are values *below which a* does not extend. For instance, we saw that Austin would give a minimal value to a; where the t elements were connoted by a single verb, a would usually be only a small fraction of t. We argued that this account was unsound. Doing X may involve producing the muscular contractions p, q, and r, and so in some sense 'doing' p, q, and r; but for most contexts, p, q, r, and X are not four concurrent or consecutive discrete 'acts', nor one act followed by three consequences. In most contexts it is not appropriate to say, as Austin would, that 'doing X' is a misnomer for 'doing p, q, and r, with the consequence X';

one is doing X. X is the act-term, and p, q, and r would be at most elements in the act-definition.

Second, there is a wide range of values *within which a* may vary. The line between 'act' and 'consequences' may often be drawn at several different places; 'doing X with the consequence Y' may often be re-described, or alternatively described, as 'doing Y'; the act-term may often be elided without trace into the term which denotes the consequence of the act; we may say that Macbeth stabbed Duncan and, as a consequence, killed him: but we may also simply say that he killed him.

Third, there are values *above which a* does not extend; that is, there are some act-terms which can *not* be elided into the corresponding consequence-description. In making this suggestion, I broach my third thesis concerning the distinction between 'act' and 'consequences'.

The trend of suggestions such as those of Professor Smart, quoted above, would rather lead to denying this contention. They would give a maximal value to a; indeed, if the saving of the four negroes' lives were looked on as the final consequence, we should have

$$t - a = 0;$$

there would be no point at which a line could be drawn between 'act' and 'consequence'. Since the sheriff encompassed the one man's death in order to save the lives of four others, Smart suggested that it would be quite proper to re-describe his act as 'saving four lives'. Just as the description, 'singing a song', may be elided into the description, 'entertaining people', and the latter description shows no trace of the former, because the latter was a consequence of the former: so the description of the sheriff's act, 'committing judicial murder', would be elided without trace into the description, 'saving four lives', since that was the consequence of the murder.

In discussions of the moral evaluation of an act, the importance of such re-descriptions is considerable. An apologist for killing people who are suffering from incurable diseases may say that such an act is 'really just putting an end to the unfortunate people's suffering'; Dr. Verwoerd said that he would 'really describe *apartheid* as good neighbourliness'. St. Paul said that one must not lie, even in order to promote the glory of God; but if an act may always be re-described in terms of its consequences, then the act of the person who told lies so high-mindedly could be re-described simply as 'promoting the glory of God'. Such suggestions have macabre possibilities. Imperious Caesar, dead and turned to clay, might stop a hole to keep the wind away; but if our formula holds for all values of *a*, killing him with that end in view might be re-described simply as 'blocking a draught'.

Hence the importance of the contention that there are values *above which a* does not extend. Our third thesis takes up that contention.

Thesis Three: Certain kinds of act are of such significance that the terms which denote them may not, special contexts apart, be elided into terms which (a) *denote their consequences, and* (b) *conceal, or even fail to reveal, the nature of the act itself.* Typical examples are the acts of killing, maiming, slandering, torturing, deceiving, or seriously offending another person; betraying or deserting a friend or an ally; breaking a contract or a promise or a confidence; stealing or destroying or spoiling something which the owner, or the community, looks on as precious; sacrificing or endangering one's own life, happiness, good name, health, or property. For instance, 'Macbeth stabbed Duncan and, as a consequence, killed him', may be re-described simply as, 'Macbeth killed Duncan'; but, 'Macbeth killed Duncan and, as a consequence, succeeded him', may not be re-described simply as, 'Macbeth succeeded Duncan'. To quote a more recent example, it was alleged during the Eichmann trial that a Nazi research institute asked a concentration-camp commandant to supply it with a number of infant bodies for use in some experiments, and that in order to comply with this request the commandant had the required number of babies of Jewish women prisoners gassed. Now to describe his act as 'assisting medical research', or 'promoting the advancement of science', simply would not do, even though research may have been assisted or scientific knowledge advanced as a result of his act. Taking human life, we feel, is an act of such significance that one cannot elide its description into a term which denotes its consequence, or an end to which it was a means, unless that term makes clear that this was the means used. Had the commandant gassed the children in order to comply with Hitler's decree that the Jewish people were to be destroyed, it might not be altogether inaccurate to subsume his act under some such description as 'genocide'; though perhaps the relation of particular murders to a policy of genocide is not that of act to consequence, or of means to end, but of part to whole.

This thesis, then, is supplementary to the theses that several alternative descriptions of a given act are possible, and that one may often, in analysing a given incident, draw the line between 'act' and 'consequences' now at one point, now at another. It holds that in certain cases there is one point at least at which an 'act'/'consequences' line *must* be drawn. The previous thesis is exemplified by the fact that 'A told B an untruth with the consequence that B was deceived' may be re-described as simply, 'A deceived B'; the present thesis is exemplified by the fact that 'A deceived B with the consequence that he won his vote' may not be re-described simply as 'A won B's vote'. In the terms of the twelve contemplated descriptions of the sheriff's act, Number 1 ('He tensed his finger') usually *should* be elided into one of the latter descriptions, e.g. Number 9 ('He shot a man');

similarly, Number 9 may be elided into Number 10 ('He killed a man'). But Number 10 may not be elided into Number 12 ('He saved four lives'); an 'act'/'consequences' line must be drawn between Numbers 10 and 12. Tensing one's finger is simply part of the act of shooting, or shooting a man; but killing a man is not simply part of the act of saving four lives. It might be objected that each is a means to an end: tensing the forefinger a means, firing the gun the end; killing one man a means, saving four others the end. But for one thing, this overlooks the fact that a means is often an act, and that an act is often a means. Furthermore, even if killing a man is intended by the agent, and characterized by an observer, simply as a means to an end, it is a means whose nature must be clearly revealed in any normal account of what was done. It is true that there are many cases in which the particular way of obtaining a certain result is of no particular interest or significance at all; in those cases, to which our previous thesis applied, the description of the act by which the result was achieved may quite properly be absorbed into the description of the result itself. We may even hesitate in such cases to make any 'act'/'consequence' distinction, and feel that this was simply one of several possible ways of doing the same thing. Perhaps my gas-fire's being alight is, as it happens, a consequence of my putting a match to it; but the same result would have been achieved by using a cigarette-lighter, or a built-in spring-and-flint device; and it is usually sufficient to say, 'I lit the gas-fire.' There is no need to specify the nature of the act by which I did so, unless it was *either* of peculiar interest in a *special* context: as might be the case, for instance, when an experiment was being made for commercial purposes with some new gadget for flameless, sparkless, lighting; *or* unless the act was of such a nature as to be of great significance in *any* normal context: for instance, because I used a rare and precious manuscript with which to light the fire.

Some elements of an incident, then, may figure merely as part of an act-description, not themselves demanding specific mention or characterization or manifestation when the incident is described, the term which denotes them being elided into the act-description, or into a consequence-description. But some elements, or combinations of elements, are such that, whenever they are present, they verify an autonomous act-definition. They constitute an instance of some kind of act whose description, special contexts apart, cannot be absorbed into some other: that 'other' remains a consequence of the act, not a part of it: extrinsic, not intrinsic, to it. They constitute a 'case' of morally significant action. Moral discourse has a well-developed vocabulary of terms denoting such cases. This is not peculiar to moral discourse, however, and it will be useful to notice some of the features of 'case-terms' in general.

Most departments of human discourse provide themselves with terms which are of convenience and utility for identifying acts, occurrences, situations, processes, phenomena, or in general 'cases', which are of special importance for their particular disciplines or interests. In games, for example, there are terms in which the rules lay down obligatory and forbidden actions and moves, methods of scoring, penalties, criteria for winning and losing; but quite apart from these, other terms come to be used to characterize certain types of action, move, or situation. Thus in tennis, the rules use such terms as 'serve', 'fault', 'game', and 'set'; but players, spectators, and commentators also speak of 'smash', 'volley', 'drive', 'lob', and—what is rather different—'ace'. The same thing is found in the sciences, both pure and applied. In medicine, for instance, there is a highly developed vocabulary denoting kinds of disease, distinct from each other, and individually identifiable with greater or less readiness by the presence of recognizable characteristic criteria or 'symptoms'. A mother may know simply that her child is not well; but a doctor, after discovering the characteristic symptoms, identifies the trouble as a case of, say, measles, or scarlatina, or diphtheria. Let us refer to these useful terms as 'case-terms'.

Three things in particular seem to stimulate the development of these vocabularies of case-terms in a given department of human discourse. First, an act, occurrence, process, situation, or phenomenon is noticed to be of frequent occurrence, and second, it seems to be of some importance for the interests of the department in question; if neither of these points is present, terms are slow to develop. It happens occasionally in tennis that a ball hits the net-tape and runs along it before falling to the ground, and it happens quite commonly that a player bounces the ball before serving, but neither of these cases bears any particular name; the first is presumably too rare, and the second too unimportant, for anyone to have felt the need to devise terms for them. Third, the act or event in question comes to be identified as conforming to a certain pattern, and hence as being an instance or case of a recurring type or kind or class, and a case-term is devised accordingly. The logic of case-terms raises many problems which do not concern us here; it is enough for us to remark that their existence has two advantages which bear on our present inquiry.

First, the constituent elements, or at any rate the necessary and sufficient conditions for application, of a case-term may often be defined with a considerable degree of accuracy; they therefore have the technical advantage of helping us to identify 'cases' with some precision, and the linguistic advantage of compendiousness. A case-term, often a single word, enables the speaker to indicate, and the listener to infer, a number of important points. For instance, if we are told that a tennis-player hit a 'smash', we know (1) that he played an overhead shot (2) with an action resembling that of serving, (3) that it was not the first stroke of the rally, i.e. the serve itself, and almost certainly (4) not the second, i.e.

the return of service. Again, if a chemist reports that a process has proved to be a case of 'catalysis', then we know that he means (1) that a chemical change has taken place, and (2) that the change has been accelerated; and that the acceleration has been brought about (3) not by merely physical means, such as increased temperature or reduced pressure, but (4) by the presence of an additional chemical substance, which (5) did not itself undergo permanent chemical change.

A second advantage is that the presence of the appropriate distinctive features, say p, q, and r, may help establish that a case of, say, X is present; then from this in turn one may be able to conclude to the presence of certain other features, a, b, c. These latter may be of greater logical generality than p, q, and r, or they may be of special practical or speculative significance. Suppose that the symptoms p, q, and r are known to be found if, and only if, a case of diphtheria is present; then a doctor discovering these symptoms knows, not only that this is a case of diphtheria, but also that the disease is infectious and that quarantine measures must be taken. Furthermore, the features a, b, and c, whose presence is inferred from the presence of a case of X, are sometimes predicates of evaluative, or quasi-evaluative, force. If it is said that a tennis-player hit a 'smash', we know that the three or four features mentioned above are present; but we do not know that the stroke won the point for the player, nor even that it did not lose it for him: a smash may be returned, or it may go 'out', or into the net. However, if it is said that the player hit an 'ace', we not only know that he served into court, but also that his opponent failed to return, or even touch, the serve, and hence that the server won the point. One might therefore call 'ace' a quasi-evaluative term; if all the elements of its definition have been verified, then the serve has been 'good': and indeed, not only legally good, i.e. 'in' as the rule requires, but performed so successfully that the point has been won.

Now moral discourse has a rich and flexible vocabulary of case-terms, which displays features similar to those of other departments of human discourse. Presumably the same things stimulated its development. The essential features of morally significant behaviour and situations constantly recur in recognizable patterns which usually enable even the most originally contrived deeds to be subsumed under the traditional case-terms, which have been fashioned because of the frequent occurrence of such deeds, and the special importance they have for human happiness and welfare. Moral case-terms bear witness to the fact that, despite the human ingenuity for devising new ways of practising the old virtues and vices, most morally significant behaviour still instantiates those virtues and vices.

These terms offer both the advantages of other case-terminologies. First, the necessary and sufficient conditions for their application are fairly accurately defined, and hence convey a number of points quite compendiously. For instance, one ascribes to A the *theft* of B's x if and only if (1) A took x; (2) x did not belong to him, but to B; (3) he did not return to it B, but consumed, sold, destroyed (or abandoned?) it; (4) B had not given A leave for this action. Moral case-terms are commonly both precise and concise. Second, these terms are commonly associated with the ordinary predicates of moral evaluation. When one sets out on the moral evaluation of an act, one does not begin each time from first principles, but seeks to identify it as an instance of some kind of act, it being agreed that acts of that kind are good, or bad, or wrong, or requiring justification, or the like. Suppose that p, q, and r are the distinctive elements in the definition of the case-term X, which denotes a kind of act agreed to be wrong; then given that one descries the presence of p, q, and r in a given individual act, one identifies it as a case of X, and accordingly judges it to be wrong, without any recourse to first principles. X plays rather the role of a middle term in a syllogism or sorites.

These case-terms, then, refer to different *kinds* of act. To avoid discussion of whether the most appropriate term is 'kind', or 'type', or 'class', or some other word used in modern books of logic, let us adapt a suggestion of Bentham. In his long Chapter 16, he sets out to give an exhaustive division of legal offences, and in some interesting footnotes (pp. 204–7) suggests the method *per genus et differentiam*: working down from *genera superiora*, one eventually arrives at the *species* by adding the *differentia specifica*. 'Species' is quite a useful term; and since our interest is with moral, not legal, evaluation, and with good deeds as well as bad, let us say that the instances of one of these recognizable kinds of act constitute a 'moral species', and call the corresponding case-terms 'moral-species-terms', or simply *species-terms*. These terms are often single words, such as 'murder', 'mayhem', 'rape', 'adultery', 'theft', 'calumny', 'lying', 'perjury', 'almsgiving'; sometimes they are phrases, such as 'breach of promise', 'breach of contract'.

There are many terms of wider extension: for instance, 'unchastity', 'dishonesty', 'justice', 'charity', and so on. These frequently embrace a number of species. 'Unchastity', for example, embraces 'adultery', 'rape', 'incest', and so on. 'Dishonesty' is of even wider extension; it includes 'lying', with its sub-species such as 'perjury' and 'calumny', and 'theft', with its sub-species such as 'embezzlement' and 'robbery'; 'fraud', 'forgery', and 'cheating' may come under both 'lying' and 'theft', and 'hypocrisy' not quite under either, though it will involve some sort of dishonesty. Bentham speaks of *genera* of offences; we may therefore call these terms *genus-terms*. They differ from species-terms in some interesting ways. For one thing, very few species-terms are available to denote acts that are thought to be good, or commendable; but there are many genus-terms which apply to good behaviour. Genus-terms frequently have opposites in a way that species-terms have not: we have 'honesty' and 'dishonesty', 'chastity' and 'unchastity', 'justice' and 'injustice', and so on; but there are no corresponding opposites for 'theft', or 'rape', or 'calumny'. Furthermore, both these types of term commonly have a noun-form and an adjective-form; but, when expressing an opinion about an act, we more commonly use the noun-form of a species-term, and the adjective-form of a genus-term; that is, we are more likely to say, 'That was a lie', or 'That was murder', than to say, 'That was mendacious', or 'That was murderous': but we more naturally say, 'That was dishonest', or 'That was unjust', than 'That was dishonesty', or 'That was injustice' (or even 'an act, or a case, of dishonesty or injustice'). It would be interesting to pursue this, if we were engaged in a wider study of the language and logic of moral evaluation; genus-terms seem to be much less 'descriptive' and much more 'evaluative', and they lend themselves much more readily to the function of predicate than do species-terms; and an investigation of the reasons why this is so might be illuminating. For our own purpose, however, it is enough to notice that a rich, flexible, and often well-defined vocabulary of moral-species-terms is accepted and used, both in ordinary and philosophical language. The fact that they are so frequently nouns, or at least noun-phrases, fits them very well to serve as act-terms in the sense that our thesis requires.

It is to the acts denoted by the species-terms that this, our Thesis Three, particularly applies. The following points need to be made concerning the thesis.

1. The first concerns the proviso, 'special contexts apart', in the statement of the thesis. We do not use sense-datum terms for the ordinary language of material-object perception, but may do so in some special contexts; we may have occasion to say to an optician, for instance, 'I see four black marks on a white surface', instead of the usual 'I see the word "Stop"'. Similarly, though rejecting Austin's definition of an act as a muscular contraction, we noticed that there are

nevertheless special contexts in which the appropriate answer to the question, 'What did he do?', will be given in terms of muscular contraction. The question arises, then, whether there may also be special contexts in which species-terms, which in normal circumstances are non-elidable, may be elided into the description of the particular consequences. It might be suggested, for instance, that a person is interested solely in some technical aspect of the incident, and that the general human significance of the act is accordingly beside the point. Two things may be said about this suggestion.

First, the thesis was put forward earlier that there is not necessarily one, and only one, correct description of a particular act, and two of the reasons given for that thesis may be recalled. It was suggested that the description of an act appropriate to a given occasion may vary with (a) the specialized interest of the inquirer, observer, or narrator, and (b) the specialized efforts, interests, or intentions of the agent. Now the first of these factors might conceivably warrant the non-expression of an act-term which in normal contexts is non-elidable. An economist, say, or an engineer, might give an account of the building of the Burma Railway under the Japanese during the Second World War, confining himself to the technical, economic, or mechanical aspects of the methods employed, and of their consequences, and saying nothing of the human suffering and the loss of life involved. Perhaps even this grudging concession is too liberal; even in these cases one expects a mention of the most significant human aspects of the situation, for the writer or reader of technical reports is also a human being; still, I do not think that the purposes of our present discussion demand that it be entirely ruled out of court. A similar concession seems quite impossible, however, on the other score, viz. the specialized interests or intentions of the agent. Suppose that a certain kind of act-term is non-elidable, because its analysis includes the elements a, b, and c. Those aspects of the act are not removed by the fact that the agent claims to be interested only in the elements *d*, *e*, and *f*. Whatever be the elements on which his attention is focused, he performs the act which contains all six elements; and by hypothesis, any act which contains the elements *a*, *b*, and *c* is non-elidable, and any account of what is done must make it clear, for normal hearers at least, that these elements are present. One might imagine Nero protesting that he was concerned with his palace illuminations solely from the aesthetic point of view, and hence was simply not interested in the point that the act of which the illuminations were a consequence was the burning of living Christians. This would be as inept as a protest by Shylock that he was concerned with his contract solely from the legal point of view, and hence was not interested in the consequences of the act by which the contract was to be honoured.

But second, even if one were to grant the possibility of such exceptions because of the special point of view taken in a particular context, that would not affect our own discussion: for a 'special point of view' is not that to which moral judgement addresses itself. By hypothesis, the special point of view would be one which prescinded from matters affecting the welfare of ourselves and others; and such a point of view is precisely not that of moral investigation. To omit to mention aspects of an act which were of 'particular human significance' would be to fail to provide the very data which we are concerned to seek: the circumstances of an act which are relevant to its moral evaluation. This, as we shall soon notice, is not to say that the act is necessarily wrong, or right, simply because these elements are present: but it is to say that no moral evaluation of it is possible unless these elements are taken into account, and hence first shown to be present.

2. To put forward the present thesis is not to deny that non-elidable *act*-terms may often serve to denote the *consequences* of the act under a narrower description. If what A does to B is the non-elidable Y, which has the consequence

Z, then by hypothesis A's act cannot be described as 'doing Z'; but Y may often be given as the consequence of X, his act under some narrower description. For instance, 'killing B' may be given as the description of A's *act*, a description which may not be elided into such descriptions as 'succeeding to B's title', or 'inheriting B's fortune'; but 'killing B' may also be given as a *consequence* of his act described as 'discharging a fire-arm in a public place', or 'careless driving'. The harm or discomfort or inconvenience which A causes B may be *part* of his act under one description, e.g. 'maim', or 'frighten', or 'anger', or 'insult'; but it may be a *consequence* of the act under another description, e.g. 'strike', 'threaten', 'jostle', or 'criticize'.

3. To put forward this thesis is to make a different point from that made by Miss Anscombe concerning a series of statements, referring to a given act, in which there is a break beyond which the statements do not answer the question, 'What is he doing?', but the question, 'What is he doing it for?'[1] She considers the case of a man who is pumping water into a cistern which supplies the drinking-water of a house regularly inhabited by the chiefs of a tyrannical ruling party who are bent on destroying the Jewish people; another person has satisfied himself that if they are killed some good men will come to power who will govern well, and even institute the Kingdom of Heaven on earth, and secure a good life for all the people; accordingly he has poisoned the water, and revealed to the man who is pumping both the fact of having laid the poison and the anticipated consequences. If a third person comes on the scene, question and answer might then run as follows: 'Why are you moving your arm up and down?' 'To work the pump.' 'Why are you doing that?' 'To fill the cistern with poisoned water.' 'Why do that?' 'To poison the party-chiefs.' 'Why kill them?' 'To save the Jews, and to bring the other group to power.' 'Why put them in?' 'To institute the Kingdom of Heaven on earth.'

[1] *Intention* (Oxford, 1957), pp. 37–47.

Concerning such a series of questions and answers, Miss Anscombe makes two points rather like my own. First, she remarks that in many cases where one can say, 'I am doing X in order to do Y', one can also say, 'I am doing Y': for instance, one could say with equal propriety either, 'I am working the pump in order to replenish the water-supply', or 'I am replenishing the water-supply'. She speaks of the description of the means as being 'swallowed up' by the description of the end; which is rather like my own point, that in many cases the description of the act may be 'elided' into the description of the act's consequences. Second, she points out that in the series there comes a 'break', beyond which the statements will serve as an answer to the question, 'Why is he doing that?', but not to the question, 'What is he doing?' Such answers as 'Replenishing the water-supply', or 'Poisoning the party-chiefs', may, on occasion, be answers to either question; but 'Instituting the Kingdom of Heaven on earth', or 'Saving the Jews', will not do as answers to the question, 'What is he doing?', but only to 'Why is he doing that?' As Miss Anscombe says, there is a break in the series, beyond which the 'swallowing-up' cannot be done; and this sounds a little like my own contention that, in many cases, the description of the act cannot be elided into the description of the consequences.

However, her point and mine differ in at least two respects. For one thing, she is speaking only of intentional action; whereas my own thesis, as we shall see in a moment in (4), also applies to acts which are unintended, and consequences which are unforeseen, by the agent. But the second difference is more important: Miss Anscombe is making a point about certain *end*-terms. She is holding that some terms which describe an agent's end or aim are not appropriate answers to the question, 'What is he doing?' She gives no rule to guide us about the place at which we may expect the break to occur, nor any account of why it is that some statements in the series will serve as answers to either question, others only to one. In some cases, of course, there is a simple chronological reason: if one is doing X so that Y may happen, it often cannot be said that one is doing Y if X and Y are widely separated in time. Sometimes the consequence-term may be given, albeit a trifle rhetorically, as an account of what the agent *is doing*, or, ironically, as an account of what he *was doing*, though it will not serve as a statement of what he *did*: for instance, a politician may say of a soldier, or the soldier may say of himself, that he was 'making a world fit for heroes to live in'; but one could not say that that was what he did, or that that was his act, at a given time, as one could say of him that he rescued a wounded man from No-Man's-Land, or captured an enemy machine-gun post. But sometimes the chronological reason will be sufficient to prevent one's re-describing 'He did X so that Y might happen' even as 'He was doing Y'. A consequence of a satirist's writing a book may be that his victims will be outraged; but one could hardly say that, during the days of composition, he was outraging them. In some cases, however, there is more than the simple chronological reason. The concept 'act' seems to involve a certain particularity, and applies to a comparatively restricted number of terms; whereas 'end' embraces both these particular terms, and many terms of considerable generality. Some terms which denote reasons-for-acting are too general to serve as act-terms; they may denote typical objects of βούλησις, but are not sufficiently particular to denote objects of προαίρεσις: 'Instituting the Kingdom of Heaven on earth' is usable as an end-term, but not as an act-term; 'Poisoning the party-chiefs' is usable as either. Here then is the difference: Miss Anscombe's is a point concerning certain end-terms: that they will not (because of their excessive generality, or for some other reason) serve as act-terms; whereas my own is a point concerning certain act-terms: that they may not, because of the particular human significance of the acts they denote, be elided into terms which denote the end of the agent or the consequence of the act.

4. To put forward this thesis is not to say that the only cases in which 'doing X with the consequence Y' may not be re-described as 'doing Y' are those in which X is a moral-species-term, nor that the only reason for the non-elidability of X is the great human significance of acts of this kind. A more general point seems to be that X is elidable into Y to the extent that Y is the *anticipatable* consequence of an act such as X.

On the one hand, of course, this is not to say that Y must be anticipated by the agent as the consequence of his doing X. It is true that in many cases where elision is appropriate, Y is the intended (and therefore anticipated) consequence of doing X: in other words, the original description, 'doing X with the consequence Y', might equally be given as, 'doing X *in order that* Y': thus, Macbeth stabbed Duncan in order to kill him; A told B an untruth in order to deceive him; the person flicked the switch in order that the light might go on; the singer sang to the people in order to entertain them. But anticipation of the consequence is neither a necessary nor a sufficient condition of the act-description's elidability into the consequence-description. It is not necessary, for we frequently make the elision in cases when the agent does not anticipate the consequence which his act brings about: if a passenger speaks to a bus-driver and thus distracts him, we may say simply that he distracted him, even though he had not intended or foreseen such an eventuality; if a person plugs in an electric radiator, and as a result overloads the circuit and fuses the wiring of the house, we may say simply that he fused it, although he anticipated no such result. It is not a sufficient condition, for the elision of the act-description is not made when the act is known not to be having its intended consequence: for example, if a singer is in fact irritating or boring his hearers, it would be ironical to say, 'He is entertaining them'; and Miss Anscombe remarks that, if an observer knows that the water being pumped by the man in her example is pouring out of a hole in the pipe on the way to the cistern, we should say 'He is replenishing the water-supply' only as a joke.

On the other hand, one does not make the elision if the consequence is completely unexpected, even by the observer: 'doing X with the consequence Y' is not re-described as 'doing Y', if there is no reason to think that this sort of act, X, will have this sort of consequence, Y. For example, if the consequence of a man's switching on the light is that he is killed (say, by a fault in the wiring), one cannot re-describe his act simply as 'He killed himself.' As a result of lying back in his bath and seeing the water-level rise, Archimedes is said to have discovered his famous principle; but one could not re-describe that homely act as 'discovering the Principle of Displacement'. Such consequences are not to be antici-pated as generally, or naturally, following from such acts. The point seems to hold for cases where, although it is sub-sequently discovered that a certain kind of act produces a certain kind of consequence, it is not known at the time of acting. Röntgen put a book with a key in it between a sample of pitch-blende and a photographic plate and, as a result, obtained an X-ray photograph of the key. We would now expect such a result from such an act; but no one at the time could do so, and it would not do to re-describe Röntgen's act then as 'taking an X-ray photograph of a key'.

Rather, we elide the act-term X into the consequence-term Y when Y is the kind of consequence that may be antici-pated from an act of the kind X: when, that is, Y is naturally, on general grounds, *anticipatable* by the agent or informed observer. 'Macbeth stabbed Duncan in order to kill him' may be re-described as 'Macbeth killed Duncan', because the victim's death is an anticipatable consequence of such an act; and for corresponding reasons one may elide the act-description in 'A told B an untruth in order to deceive him', 'He flicked the switch with the result that the light went on', and 'He sang to the people in order to entertain them'. This also applies to 'The passenger spoke to the driver and, as a result, distracted him': the passenger may not have intended or foreseen that result, but the other passengers could readily anticipate it on quite general grounds; such a consequence may be expected from such an act.

This helps to account for two points. First, the more remote a consequence, the slower we are to re-describe an act in terms of it. No doubt the creation of Czecho-Slovakia in 1920 was a remote consequence of Prinzip's shooting the Archduke Francis Ferdinand at Sarajevo in 1914; but it was not a consequence that one could anticipate from such an act, and one could not re-describe Prinzip's act as 'creating Czecho-Slovakia'. Second, the point accounts for cases where it is natural to describe a person who is doing X as *trying* to do Y (a possible consequence of X), but not as doing Y. We stress the *trying* when we anticipate that non-success is very, or quite, likely; the task is delicate, or intricate, or laborious, and people who do X in the hope of effecting Y frequently fail to do so. A man whose car is giving trouble, and who has to ask some friends to push it in an attempt to start it 'on the run', will be described as 'trying to start his car'; whereas the act of pressing the starter-button in normal circumstances is called simply 'starting the car'. There are some words in which the 'trying' element is implicit and need not be expressed; a doctor is often said to be 'treating' a patient, i.e. attempting to cure him: not 'curing' him, nor 'trying to treat' him. We may notice that the agent who is doing X in order that Y may happen says, 'I am trying to do Y', only if he has some doubts about his likely success; otherwise he says, 'I am doing Y': though subsequently, should he (to his surprise) fail, he will say, 'I was trying to do Y', but not, 'I was doing Y'.

An attempt might be made to account for the non-elidability of moral-species-terms by reference to the test of anticipatability. One may re-describe 'Macbeth stabbed Duncan in order to kill him' as 'Macbeth killed Duncan', because one may anticipate on general grounds that such an act will have such a consequence; but one cannot re-describe 'Macbeth killed Duncan in order to succeed him' as 'Macbeth succeeded Duncan', for such a consequence does not generally follow from such an act: stabbers commonly kill, but killers do not commonly succeed to thrones. However, such an attempt is beyond the scope of our essay; so we may come to the final point concerning this Thesis Three.

5. To put forward this thesis is not to espouse any one particular ethical theory; people may concur in subscribing to it, but differ widely when they come to give a rationale of moral-species-terms.

As Mill says, people who are agreed about specific moral judgements frequently disagree about the first principles of morals: disagree, for instance, in explaining how it is that a particular species-term comes to be associated with a particular predicate of moral evaluation, and in giving a philosophical validation of such predications. For Aquinas, for instance, a given kind of act comes to be judged right or wrong, good or bad, by rational reflection on its harmony or disharmony with one or other of the three fundamental aspects of human nature: substantial, animal, rational. But Aquinas does not expect us to initiate this reflection from the beginning whenever we evaluate an individual act; he expects us to subsume the act under the appropriate moral 'species', to which one of the different evaluative predicates applies. Kant would test, if not actually determine, the morality of an act by reference to the principle of universalizability, or to very general maxims such as 'Always treat persons as ends, never solely as means'; but the task is simplified by the recognition of moral rules which set out our duties in much more specific terms. For Bentham, an act is to be approved or disapproved according as it does or does not conform with the Principle of Utility, and promises to produce greater pleasure or pain. But he does not expect us to undertake the calculus from scratch on each occasion; he arranges acts, or at any rate offences, into a series of 'species' which takes him more than a hundred pages to set out. Between the very general first principle or primary precept, then, whether it be 'Follow Nature', 'Maximize pleasure', or 'Act only on that maxim whereby thou canst at the same time will that it should become a universal law', and the individual judgement, 'It was wrong of Jones to do that', there come such specific evaluations as 'Murder is wrong'; in such theories, these specific evaluatons are logically intermediate between the other two. In Intuitionist theories they are not derived from, or validated by reference to, principles logically prior to them, but are seen immediately to be true. But however one accounts for them, the specific judgements have the two advantages of being easily manipulated, and commanding wide agreement. The terms in which they are couched are familiar, and fairly well defined. When Bentham sets out on his classification of offences into their species and genera, he grumbles that it is 'the fate of science, and particularly of the moral branch, that the distribution of things must in great measure be dependent on their names: arrangement, the work of mature reflection, must be ruled by nomenclature, the work of popular caprice'. But the fortunate thing is that Bentham, in the event, and most moral theorists have alike anticipated Hampshire's advice, that any attempt to discover and classify the essential human virtues should be guided at every point by the ordinary terms and divisions which have been found useful in human experience, and already recognized and marked in the vocabulary of the language; and this holds especially for the terms which we have been calling moral-species-terms.

Of course, one must not imply that there is unanimous agreement on every detail of the definition and identification and evaluation of all these species-terms. Two people may say, 'Lying is always wrong', but not be in such full agreement as that would suggest. One may mean, 'It is always wrong, in all circumstances, to tell an untruth'; the other may mean, 'It is not wrong to tell an untruth in circumstances where this is the only way to avoid breaking a confidence; but then, in those circumstances, I should not call it "lying".' The latter person would, oddly enough, frequently be in more substantial agreement with a person who says, 'In some circumstances lying is not wrong.' It is not always easy to identify the cause of such disagreements. They may arise because one person holds, and the other denies, that there are kinds of act which are wrong, or forbidden, in all circumstances. For Aquinas, some kinds of act are 'intrinsically evil'; for Kant, there are some 'duties of perfect obligation'; whereas for Bentham, 'every action whatsoever' is to be approved or disapproved in the light of the Principle of Utility. But the difference may also arise because, though each agrees that 'Lying is wrong', they give different definitions of 'lie' according to the differences in their general ethic. Aquinas, testing acts by their conformity to the ends and capacities and inclinations of the human person, considers that the essence of a lie consists in its running counter to the end of the faculty of speech, viz. to communicate to others what is in one's mind; hence his definition of a lie as *Locutio contra mentem*: whenever that definition is fulfilled the speaker is guilty of a lie, whether the hearer is deceived or not. Bentham, however, sees the wrongfulness of any act in its tendency to produce harmful consequences; if therefore on a given occasion there is no danger of one's hearer being deceived, there is no lie. Borderline disagreements, however, do not alter the large area of agreement which is sufficient for our thesis, and they draw attention to another point of general ethical theory on which people who subscribe to the thesis may yet disagree.

To put forward this thesis is not necessarily to imply, with Aquinas and Kant, that there are certain kinds of act which are always morally wrong, never permissible in any circumstances. It is not to lay down some rigid rule for the moral evaluation of a given kind of act, but to say something about its characterization in moral discourse. The point is not that these acts are so wicked that sound moral judgement must always condemn them, but that they are so significant for human existence and welfare and happiness that they must always be taken into account before sound moral judgement can be passed on them; and if they are to be taken into account, their presence must first be revealed. The feature of non-elidability applies, therefore, not only to terms such as 'murder', 'mayhem', and 'betrayal', into which some sort of moral judgement is built, but also to terms like 'kill', 'maim', and 'deceive', which may be purely factual and descriptive. If one were asked one's opinion of the morality of an episode described as 'A did X', which failed to inform one that A's doing X first involved his killing, grieving, maiming, or deceiving some other person, one would naturally complain that one had been denied data necessary for reaching a sound verdict.

The thesis is therefore compatible with a theory which, though conceding that there are grounds—and indeed *moral* grounds—for distinguishing between various *kinds* of act, holds nevertheless that any kind of act may be justified if only there are sufficiently happy consequences in prospect if it is done, or sufficiently unpleasant consequences if it is not. Bentham's is an excellent case in point. He insists that every action whatsoever should be approved or disapproved according to its tendency to produce or prevent pleasure or pain, and considers any departure from this norm as rueful evidence that 'Such is the stuff that man is made of: in principle and in practice, in a right track and in a wrong one, the rarest of all human qualities is consistency.' He thinks that, in general, the combination of an act and the relevant 'criminative' circumstances constitutes, because of its tendency to produce harmful consequences, a certain offence; but this may always be set aside when other, 'modifying', circumstances supervene. By this, however, he does not mean that they alter the characterization appropriate to the action, in the sense that it is no longer a case of X, but now of Y or Z; he means that they alter the verdict to be passed on the act or the agent: it is still a case of X, but in the special circumstances, doing X may be excused or justified. 'In some circumstances', he says, 'even to kill a man may be a beneficial act'; but he does not suggest that it should no longer be described as 'killing a man'. Where there are 'modifying' circumstances, as he calls them, it is the evaluation which may be modified, not the description. Indeed Bentham, thoroughgoing Utilitarian though he was, seems to have been the last philosopher to have attempted to give a logically exhaustive division and classification of the kinds, or 'species', of act which constitute offences, 'as much for moral discourse as for legislative practice'. The terms which denote these species are a typical, and for our present purpose the most important, class of the terms which have here been called 'non-elidable'. It is of them particularly that I want to say, not that moral judgement must always pronounce them wrong: but that whenever their definition is verified they must be characterized in isolation before moral judgement can be passed on the whole incident of which they are part. Perhaps they are not always morally wrong; but they are always morally significant. There will be much wider agreement about what kinds of act are morally significant than about the moral significance of each.

§ 2. ACTS OF OMISSION

Most of the examples of acts which we have so far discussed have been things which people have *done*. But moral investigation is often concerned with things which some person has *not* done, or has 'omitted' to do. We must therefore pay some attention now to Acts of Omission. In this chapter they are important in their own right, since we are inquiring about the things that count as acts; but they also shed a little further light on the questions we have been considering about 'act' and 'consequences'.

Bentham begins his study of human actions in general by distinguishing between positive acts, or acts of commission, and negative acts, or acts of omission; but he appears to have some trouble in giving a criterion for the distinction, and for deciding when one is guilty of a moral offence by way of commission and when by way of omission. The latter question is easily settled in pluralist theories such as those of Kant or Ross, or from a code such as the Decalogue: one sins by commission if one does what the code forbids, and by omission if one fails to do what the code enjoins. Bentham's monist Utilitarianism gives a criterion for deciding what is a morally bad act, viz., what hinders pleasure or produces pain; but how are we to decide whether it is an act of commission or of omission? Not, it would seem, from the 'Thou-shalt' or 'Thou-shalt-not' form of the particular precept or principle which has been contravened, for there is only one principle. He gives us the more fundamental criterion of physical activity or movement:

By positive (acts) are meant such as consist in motion or exertion: by negative, such as consist in keeping at rest; that is, in forbearing to move or exert oneself in such and such circumstances. Thus, to strike is a positive act: not to strike on a certain occasion, a negative one. Positive acts are styled also acts of commission; negative, acts of omission or forbearance.[1]

[1] p. 72.

It is a virtue of this approach that it seeks to distinguish between acts of commission and acts of omission in general, not
merely between morally wrongful deeds and omissions; and
since no recourse is had to a distinction between positive and
negative precepts, there is no inconsistency with a monist
Utilitarianism.

However, even as an account of what constitutes an
omission in general, and not merely an *immoral* omission,
I suggest that Bentham's definition will not do. To the
question, 'What were you doing at two o'clock this afternoon?', any of the following could be appropriate replies:
'Taking a siesta', 'Relaxing in an arm-chair', 'Sun-bathing',
'Sitting for a portrait', 'Waiting for the Carfax traffic lights
to change', 'Being X-rayed', 'Getting my hair cut', 'Sitting in
Whitehall in Civil Disobedience', 'Hunger-striking'. Each of
these replies would satisfy Bentham's definition of an omission as physical non-movement, 'keeping at rest'; yet we
should not call any of them an omission. Bentham's criterion
is no doubt a negative necessary condition for an omission,
but it is not a sufficient one. Before attempting to decide what
constitutes an immoral omission, therefore, we had best
investigate when it is appropriate to speak of an omission in
general, non-moral, discourse.

(i) *Omissions in general*

A person is said to have omitted X if, and only if, (1) he
did not do X, and (2) X was in some way expected of him.
Both points call for a little further explanation, for although
it is the note of 'being expected' which seems to mark off
omissions from other not-doings, some not-doing statements
refer to actions so completely unexpected that they would not
count as not-doings in any but the most artificial sense: one
hardly lists, among the things one 'did not do', such facts as
not having bought a Rolls-Royce each day last week.

   1. The same requirements for sense and appropriateness

apply to not-doing statements as apply to other negative propositions. (*a*) There are two sorts of requirement concerning the applicability of the predicate to the subject in the corresponding affirmative statement. First, the predicate must not be logically inapplicable: for a given subject, there is a range of predicates which may be meaningfully affirmed or denied of it; but if we attribute to it a predicate lying outside that range, the result is not false, but meaningless; grammatically it may be a good sentence, but logically it is not a proposition at all. Hence, just as one can meaningfully say 'This chair is not very comfortable', but not, 'This chair is not very outspoken': so one can say, 'I did not grease the Rolls-Royce', but not, 'I did not inoculate the Rolls-Royce'. Second, the predicate must not be inapplicable on the score of custom or convention—a restriction often violated by the people whom Alice met in Wonderland; or on the score of experience: it may not be logically impossible for a man to conceive and bear a child, but we know that he cannot do so; it would therefore usually be pointless to make not-doing statements to that effect. (*b*) There are also contextual requirements: there must be something in the context of a discussion or situation which gives point to making a negative statement. 'S is not P', or 'A did not X', are statements worth making only if there is some reason for thinking that the opposite is, or may be, true, or if someone has asserted, suggested, or implied that it is true, or inquired or wondered whether it is true. It is on this score that the statement, 'A did not buy a Rolls-Royce each day last week', will usually be inappropriate. However, a special context could make it natural and reasonable: it might be known that A had been commissioned by an Oil Shah to buy him a fleet of luxury cars. Not-doing statements will be appropriate only when such contextual requirements are met.

2. A's not-having-done-X is said to be an omission only if X was in some way expected of A; and that may be verified

in two ways. First, it may be expected because X is something that A usually does, or people usually do, in the situation in question. If it is a man's custom to walk down to the Post Office every day to inquire for mail, or to race his motor before turning off the ignition, or to listen to the Ten o'clock News every night, we come to expect that he will do it *this* time; hence we often say that he 'omits' the action when he does not fulfil the expectation: as we commonly do of any person who, say, does not turn off the light on his front veranda in day-time, or collect mail delivered to his letter-box. However, we are inclined to say that A 'failed' to do X only when his omission has occasioned us either disappointment on our account: e.g. 'The Queen failed to appear on the Palace balcony as she usually does'; 'The only omission in this collection which one really regrets is that of Camus's earliest articles on Algeria'; or worry on A's account: e.g. 'It was my neighbour's failure to take in his milk-bottles two days running that first made me fear he might be ill'.

Second, we also speak of A's not-doing-X as an omission when X is required of him by some rule with which he is expected to comply. This may, of course, be some moral rule, precept, or principle; but it will often be a non-moral rule. The act prescribed by the rule may be a necessary part of some function A is performing: it is an omission if a batsman does not defend his wicket against each ball he receives, but not if he does not score from it; or it may be a necessary means to some end he has chosen: prescribed, for instance, by the rule that one must switch on the microphone before making a tape-recording, or grease the pan before frying. On such occasions, and commonly, the term 'omission' will carry with it a note of disapproval; but, in non-moral discourse at least, it is not always dyslogistic. Sometimes it is neutral or non-committal, as in, 'The opening chorus, which is customary in Gilbert and Sullivan operas, is omitted in *The Yeomen of the Guard*'; or, 'Political commentators are speculating on the omission of all reference to Mr. Kozlov in Mr. Kruschev's speech last night'. Sometimes an omission may even be admired or applauded: thus, 'By omitting the usual jungle siesta and launching the raid soon after mid-day, Blamey's men caught the Japanese completely unprepared for the attack'; 'The tension of the burglary scene (in *Rififi*) was heightened by the omission of all musical accompaniment: a brilliant stroke'.

(ii) *Immoral omissions*

We are now in a position to take up the question: What is an *immoral* omission? This is not meant to include the broader question: When is an omission morally culpable? That would raise such issues as the necessity of advertence, intentionality, and foresight of consequences, for culpability; the extent to which these are conditions necessary for moral responsibility will be discussed in Chapter 3, and in this regard omissions are in no different case from positive acts. At present the question to be investigated is: Given that the conditions necessary for moral responsibility are present, when is it morally wrong of A not to have done X?

There appear to be three types of case. First, A deliberately let Y happen, when he should have prevented it; second, A did not do X, which he should have done, and the result was that Y happened; third, A did Z, which was incompatible with his doing X, and X was something which he was supposed to do. The word 'deliberately' is present only in the first case, but this does not necessarily mean that the second and third cases were involuntary, or unintentional, nor that it was only in the first case that A made a choice after weighing pros and cons. Rather, the first and second type of case differ, frequently at any rate, according to the motive that prompts the omission. In both cases A has failed to do something which he should have done, and the mischievous consequence Y has happened; but 'A deliberately let Y happen' is an idiomatic phrase indicating that Y is precisely what A wanted and sought: he deliberately refrained from taking the steps which would prevent Y, precisely in order that Y might happen. He may desire Y, either for its own sake, e.g. out of hatred or revenge, as in Agatha Christie's story where the nurse watches her patient (an unfaithful lover) in an angina attack, and gives the injection only when it is too late; or as a means to an end, as would have been the case had the injection been withheld by the patient's wife, so that she might be free to marry another man, or inherit under her husband's will. In the second type of case, Y is often something which A would prefer not to happen, but which he fails to prevent for one of several possible reasons: for instance, out of laziness— e.g. he does not want his child to contract poliomyelitis, but cannot be bothered to queue with him for Salk vaccination: or out of physical cowardice—e.g. A does not want B to drown, but fears that an attempt to rescue him may involve himself in danger; or out of moral cowardice, from fear of social or economic reprisals—e.g. he feels it his duty to oppose a measure coming up before his committee, or to support the ablest candidate for a post, but fears that his own position will be jeopardized, or his own supporters alienated, if he does so; or out of shyness—e.g. he should offer B condolence, or friendship, or encouragement, but shrinks from the embarrassment this may occasion. Similarly, in the third type of case, 'A did Z, which was incompatible with his doing X, as he was supposed to', it is not not-doing-X at which he is aiming; and if not-doing-X has some harmful consequence Y, Y may again be something which he would prefer not to have happen. For instance, a nurse is invited to a party at a time when she is on special duty; her patient seems to be peaceful, and as a result she fails to see him suffer a sudden collapse; as a consequence, he becomes dangerously ill. This third type of case differs therefore from the second, in which the omission is prompted by laziness, cowardice, and so on, in that A's reason for not doing Z is much more plainly objective-seeking; he thinks, 'I want to do Z so I am afraid I shall not be able to do X.' It differs from the first type in not being intended as a means to an end; he does not think, 'I want Y, and the way to get that is to let X happen.'

Now what is it that these three types of omissions have in common? What criteria are there for deciding whether, on a given occasion, a particular not-doing is or is not a wrongful omission? Bentham gives one sole criterion: whether or not it is productive of harmful consequences. In this, of course, he is perfectly consistent; but it is natural to object that this is not a necessary condition of an omission's being morally wrongful. The omission of an act is often blameworthy even though no harmful consequences ensue: as for instance when a mechanic fails to make a specified check on an aircraft, a nurse does not switch on the call-bell from her patient's room, or a barrister does not brief himself properly for a client's defence. Such omissions may arise from negligence, laziness, or even from malice, and we feel that they deserve censure whether the ill effects follow or not. Bentham meets such objections by arguing, on Utilitarian grounds, that censure is in place when the *probable* effects of an omission are mischievous. Even though no assignable person suffers harm, the whole community is subject to alarm and danger if such cases escape censure. But what Bentham fails to show, I think, is that the fact that not-doing-X has harmful consequences is a *sufficient* condition of its being a wrongful omission. This is not meant as an objection against his general Utilitarian ethic, but as a particular complaint about his account of omissions. He might indeed put forward a sophisticated explanation claiming to show that every wrongful omission did in fact violate the Principle of Utility; but we could still complain that his criterion is not sufficiently detailed to enable us to recognize a wrongful omission when it occurs. To see this, let us reflect for a moment on the propriety of speaking of something as a consequence of non-action. A reviewer of Mill's *System of Logic* expressed scepticism about such language, at least where it is a human agent who has not acted: the word 'cause', he suggested, applies only to that element in the antecedents of an event which 'exercises force'; it would be incorrect, he held, to say that the cause of a citadel's being taken in a surprise attack was the sentinel's being off his post.[1] But surely it is quite normal to speak of the consequence of an omission, and an omission involves some non-exercise of force. What is true, of course, is that the circumstances in which it is appropriate to say that Y is a consequence of not-doing-X are quite different from those in which it is appropriate to say that Y is a consequence of doing-X. Let us try to identify the former.

To begin with, Y is commonly said to be a consequence of A's not-doing-X when doing-X is a standard way of preventing Y, and A did not carry it out; for instance, the fact that the flowers in my garden died is said to be a consequence of my not having watered them, because if I had watered them they would not have died. But this is not enough; for although it may be true that if A had done X, Y would not have happened, it is often also true that if Tom, Dick, or Harry had done X, Y would not have happened: yet it is not said that Y is a consequence of *their* not-doing-X. Why is *A* singled out as the person whose not-doing-X caused Y? We say, 'The flowers in my garden died because I did not water them', because if I had watered them they would not have died; but if the man next door, or the milkman, had watered them, they would equally not have died; why then am *I* singled out as the one whose not watering them caused them to die? It is not that we say that the death of the flowers was also the result of these other people's not having watered them, but that they are free from blame: we do not say that the flowers' dying was a consequence of their non-action at all,

---

[1] Quoted by Mill in later editions: e.g. ed. London, 1898, p. 216 n.

blameless or otherwise; but we do say that it is a consequence of mine; why? The reason is that Y is said to be a consequence of someone's not doing X only when his not-doing-X is an *omission*; and we have found that A's not-doing-X is an omission only when doing-X is in some way *expected* of A. Y is therefore called a consequence of A's not doing X only when (1) doing X is a standard way of preventing Y, and (2) A is in some way expected to do X. Hence with the flowers: *I* am the one who is expected to water my garden; hence the death of the flowers is said to be the consequence of *my* not watering them.

This helps us make the appropriate points for moral investigation and discourse. Suppose that it is established that the harmful Y, which has happened, would not have happened if A had done X; and furthermore that X is a standard way of preventing Y. This is still not sufficient to show (1) that A's not doing X was a wrongful omission; nor (2) that it was an omission at all; nor (3) that Y may be called a consequence of A's not doing X. These conclusions would follow only if it were also established that A was expected or required— morally expected or required—to do X: i.e. that X was something which A should—morally should—have done. For instance, if A's son is not sent to school, he will suffer certain disadvantages. Those disadvantages would be obviated if A had taken the boy to school; they would also be obviated if B, a neighbour, had taken him to school. But the disadvantages are said to be a consequence only of A's not taking the boy to school, not of B's not doing so; A's not doing so is an omission, B's is not; and A's not doing so is a wrongful omission, B's is not. On the night that *Titanic* sank, the wireless operator on a ship in the vicinity went off duty at midnight, and hence did not receive the distress signal; had he done so, many lives would have been saved. But the loss of those lives cannot be called a consequence of his not having received the message; his not having done so was not a wrongful omission, nor even an omission at all: as it would have been had he failed to take such a message at 11 p.m. A motorist is not bound to stop and look to the left and right before entering a busy street if a green light assures him that he has right of way. Should it transpire that the lights have jammed, with the result that he strikes a car coming in from his right, the damage ensuing does not render his not having stopped and looked a wrongful omission, nor, again, an omission at all; and although the damage would not have been done if he had stopped and looked, it is not said to be a consequence of his not stopping and looking, since he was not required to do so. A's not having done X, then, will be called a wrongful omission only when X is something that he should, or ought to, or was supposed to, have done, i.e. when doing X was expected or required of him. To the charge 'You did not do X', it will always be a good defence to show 'I did not have to'. And if doing X would have prevented Y, Y will be called a consequence of not doing X, or of omitting to do X, only on the same condition.

This involves a further limitation. It seems to follow that A is to be held responsible, and blamed, for the harmful Y, not simply if doing X was required of him, but only if it is required of him *in order that something such as Y may not happen.* For a person can be held responsible for something only to the extent that that thing is a consequence of some action, or non-action, of his. A can therefore be held responsible for Y only to the extent that some relationship of cause and consequence exists between them; the only such relationship that exists between them is that which exists by virtue of the connexion of each with X; and, by hypothesis, X connects them only to this extent, that X is enjoined upon A in order that something such as Y may not happen. This conclusion is confirmed by ordinary moral experience. If A fails to keep an appointment with B, A is to blame for the inconvenience that B suffers as a natural result; but he is not to blame for being unavailable to help fight a fire which un-expectedly breaks out at their rendezvous; nor even for some quite unforeseen harm suffered by B, e.g. that he is knocked down by a motor-car while waiting for A: even though that would not have happened had A been on time. If an anaes-thetist does not watch the blood-pressure gauge during an operation, and hence fails to notice a weakening of the patient's heart, then he is to blame for a heart-collapse thus not prevented; but if, through not watching the gauge, he does not notice the erratic behaviour of the needle which presages a breakdown of the hospital's electric supply, he is hardly to be blamed if the breakdown occurs. The point being made here for morals is similar to that made in the legal field by jurists who hold that the extent of liability for a negligent act is confined to 'the harm within the risk', i.e. harm the likelihood of which is among the reasons for holding the act to be negligent. In moral investigations, at least, the charge that A did not do X, with the result that Y happened, will therefore be successfully rebutted if it can be shown, not only that doing X was something which was not required of A: but even that it was not required of him in order that things such as Y might not happen.

Now in what circumstances is one required to do X in order that Y may not happen? There is, of course, an im-portant sense in which one should always take opportunities to save people from suffering and misfortune when they pre-sent themselves; but if this were required in the sense that one must always perform every act in one's power which will save someone from discomfort or inconvenience, who shall 'scape whipping? The sense in which it is required may be indicated by considering the following passage from Professor Baier:

A lifeguard might say, 'I was only doing my duty', when de-clining the thanks of the lady he has rescued. A holidaymaker might, modestly, say the same. But while both are using the expression to rebut the lady's thanks, the lifeguard is speaking the truth, for it was merely his duty, and the holidaymaker is not, for it was not his duty. Of course, if there were no lifeguards and no other swimmers about, then the holidaymaker *ought* certainly to have tried to rescue her if he could swim. He deserves moral censure if he does nothing. . . . However, strictly speaking, it is merely wrong not to jump in and help her; it is not really a neglect of one's duty unless one is a lifeguard.[1]

Let us leave aside for the moment Baier's contention about the relationship of 'ought' and 'duty'; the passage is helpful in that it illustrates the two classes of case in which one *ought* to do something, and hence deserves moral censure for, and is responsible for the harmful consequences of, not doing it.

The lifeguard exemplifies one class of case, in which we may distinguish three types. First, there are the acts, activities, or functions undertaken, implicitly or explicitly, in voluntarily accepting a particular position or office or state of life; a lifeguard is at fault if he does not go to the help of swimmers who get into difficulties in his area while he is on duty; a father if he does not see to his children's education; a schoolteacher if he does not do what preparation is necessary to take a prescribed class. Second, there are the acts required by certain relationships, even though not voluntarily undertaken or entered into: that, for example, of a child to his parents, or of a citizen to his country. Third, there are acts required by particular promises of undertakings: to pay a debt, to fulfil a contract, to honour a confidence, to brief oneself for a client's defence. Special justifying circumstances apart, it is a wrongful omission if a person fails to perform an act which is required of him under one of these headings; and the harm which naturally results from not doing it will be imputed to him as a consequence of his omission.

A second class of case is exemplified by the holidaymaker; 'He deserves moral censure if he does nothing', says Baier.

---

[1] *The Moral Point of View* (Ithaca, 1958), p. 227.

This is a class of acts required or expected of one, not in virtue of any undertaking one has made, or of any *special* relationship in which one stands to another person, but by virtue of what Bentham calls 'Beneficence'. It is not a word in very common use, and no word at all suggests itself for the omissions which constitute what Bentham calls 'offences against beneficence'. We feel here acutely what may often have been felt vaguely throughout our discussions in this section: that our vocabulary of moral-species-terms is much richer for describing positive deeds than omissions. There are terms such as 'breach of promise' which apply to some of the kinds of omission which we have noted in the preceding paragraph; but for many of them there is no specific term. With this second class of omissions we are even worse off; suppose that the holidaymaker had let the swimmer drown when he could have saved her without danger to himself, who would ever describe his omission as 'a failure in beneficence', or brand his conduct as 'non-beneficent'? Still, that is no fault of Bentham's, and we may notice what he says.

He divides ethical duties into 'duties to oneself' and 'duties to one's neighbour'. The former, of course, raise many issues which moral philosophers have discussed, but it is the latter which concern us now. Of duties to our neighbour, Bentham writes:

Ethics . . . may be termed the art of discharging one's duties to to one's neighbour. Now the happiness of one's neighbour may be consulted in two ways: 1. In a negative way, by forbearing to diminish it. 2. In a positive way, by studying to increase it. A man's duty to his neighbour is accordingly partly negative and partly positive: to discharge the negative branch of it, is *probity*: to discharge the positive branch, *beneficence*.[1]

He makes it clear that he is not here including under the requirements of Beneficence those positive duties to one's neighbour which arise out of promise, office, or special

[1] p. 312.

relationship; he gives as examples cases in which one can easily save another person from injury or death without any inconvenience to oneself.[1]

Throughout this discussion I have said that a person's not-doing-X will be called a wrongful omission only when he 'ought to' or 'should', or 'was supposed to', have done X, or when X was 'required', or 'expected' of him. It might have seemed natural to bracket with these alternatives, 'only when A had an "obligation", or a "duty" to do X, or when doing-X was "obligatory" for him'. Bentham's example would encourage at least the use of the word 'duty'. So far, however, I have avoided these terms, in order not to involve my account in some recent criticisms of the way that they are often used. Baier, for instance, in the passage quoted, presupposes a point which he has argued earlier in the same chapter, viz. that those moral philosophers have been mistaken who have believed that 'obligation' is the noun corresponding to the verb 'ought'. He holds that 'A ought to do X', and 'It is wrong for A not to do X', do not entail 'A has an obligation to do X': though the latter entails each of the former. Hart has made similar points, complaining that it is absurd to speak of having a moral *duty* not to kill, or an *obligation* not to torture a child: though we certainly *ought* not do such things.[2] Both Baier and Hart agree that the terms 'obligation' and 'duty' are applicable only in cases of the first of the two classes we have distinguished, exemplified by the lifesaver. They are therefore at odds with Bentham, who would use 'duty' for both classes.

There is one point in these contentions of Baier and Hart with which I should agree: namely that, if the lifeguard had failed to go to the swimmer's rescue, we should call his failure a 'neglect of duty', or accuse him of 'dereliction of

[1] p. 323, n. 1.
[2] 'Legal and Moral Obligation', in *Essays in Moral Philosophy*, edited by A. I. Melden (Seattle, 1958), *passim*.

duty', or say of him, 'he neglected his obligations'; whereas we should not naturally apply these terms to a similar failure on the part of the holidaymaker, even in circumstances where he *should* have attempted the rescue. Such terms are appropriate only in cases of the first class which we have distinguished, and not to all of them: if a person fails to pay a debt or to keep a promise, for example, we do not say that he has been guilty of neglect, or dereliction, of duty. However, I suggest that 'One does not describe A's not-doing-X as "neglect of obligation"' does not necessarily entail 'A has no obligation to do X'. Language does not always follow such rigorous patterns. There is no guarantee that a word will retain unchanged its original sense, force, and flavour in words and phrases that are derived from it. In the new term it may acquire new overtones; as Newman points out in a similar connexion, 'inform' makes 'informer', 'adventure' makes 'adventurer', 'speculate' makes 'speculator'. A word may undergo a change of meaning when a phrase in which it is used is negated. Thus the phrase 'A has no right to do X' is not, as language is actually used, the contradictory of the phrase 'A has the right to do X'; indeed, the former is often used as almost equivalent to 'It would be wrong for A to do X': whereas the latter is by no means equivalent to 'It would be wrong for A not to do X'. Phrases such as 'neglect of duty' and 'dereliction of duty' have a much more precisely defined, and narrowly restricted, sense than have phrases such as 'having a duty to do X'. 'I have never killed anyone or stolen anything', says Baier; and he argues from this that killing and stealing are not things which one is under an obligation not to do, for, he says,

it is certainly not true that I ever discharged any obligations to Stalin or Chiang Kai-shek, for the simple reason that I never had any obligations to these gentlemen.

Against this, however, I suggest that 'I have no obligations

to A' does not entail 'I have no obligation not to do X to A';
nor does it entail 'I have no obligation to do X for A'—for
example, to save him from drowning. Words such as 'duty'
and 'obligation' may have quite a flexible and loosely defined
role in a language, and yet be taken into phrases which have
a rather technical meaning; but one cannot conclude that the
limited connotation of the technical or quasi-technical phrase
in which they figure—e.g. 'neglect of your obligations',
'dereliction of duty'—imposes similar restrictions on them
when they are used outside those phrases. Hart has urged,
in another place, that the terms 'duty' and 'obligation' should
be confined to a much more narrowly restricted 'segment of
morality'. He notes, but deplores, 'the philosophical use of
"duty" and "obligation" for all cases where there are moral
reasons for saying an action should be done, or not done'.[1]
But surely this 'philosophical use' is quite in keeping with
the ordinary language of moral experience. One may say,
'Well really, in the circumstances, I felt I just *had* to help';
but one may say, in the very same situation, 'Well really, in
the circumstances, I felt I had a *duty* to help.' Baier admits
that the holidaymaker might say to the swimmer he has
rescued, 'I was only doing my duty.' The remark would perhaps be a little pompous, but Baier's contention that the man
who made it would not be 'speaking the truth' appears a somewhat arbitrary attempt to draw rigid lines of true-and-false
in a terminology which is really quite flexible.

Bentham therefore seems to be well within his rights in
describing as our 'duties to others' things which we should,
or ought to, do or not do to others, even when they are not
required by virtue of office, voluntary undertaking, or special
relationship. He is surely speaking quite legitimately, and
certainly quite normally, in suggesting that if a woman's
head-dress catches fire, a man has a duty to try and quench

[1] 'Are there any Natural Rights?', in *Philosophical Review*, April 1955,
p. 179, n. 7.

the fire; and in suggesting—as if in anticipation of Baier's example—that if a drunkard falls face downwards into a puddle, and is in danger of drowning, a bystander has a duty at least to lift his head a little to one side and so save him. We should accordingly have been entitled throughout this discussion, it seems to me, to have said that A's not-doing-X is a wrongful omission only when, in the circumstances, A has a duty or an obligation to do X; and that, if doing-X is a standard way of preventing Y, A is to be blamed for Y's happening when he does not do X, only on the same condition.

It remains to ask in what circumstances an act is required by virtue of what Bentham calls Beneficence. Apart from the three types of case mentioned above on p. 51, when has A a duty or an obligation to do X in order that Y may not happen to B? It is difficult to determine this with much precision, and the difficulty may be connected with the fact that there is no moral-species-term in common use to characterize such cases; but four conditions seem to be necessary. First, B must be in danger of suffering significant loss of, or damage to, life or limb or liberty or happiness or good name or health or employment or material possessions. The fact that B would like some luxury—say, a new motor-car, or a holiday on the Riviera—which A could give him, and suffers disappointment when he does not get it, does not mean that A's not giving it to him is a wrongful omission, or that he is to be blamed for B's disappointment. Second, A's doing X must be necessary to prevent Y; unless there is reason to believe that no one else will do it, or if B is able to do it himself, then X is not required of A in the relevant sense. The fact that one reads in a newspaper of a baby's being orphaned does not mean that one is guilty of wrongful omission if one does not offer to adopt him, even though one is able to do so, and knows the disadvantages a child suffers if he has no home. Third, there must be a real probability that A's doing X would prevent Y; not-doing-X is not an omission if doing-X would simply be a quixotic gesture. Fourth, there must be a proportion between the harm that B is likely to suffer if A does not do X, and the harm that A is likely to suffer or the good that he is likely to jeopardize if he does. In Baier's example, the holidaymaker would have no obligation to go to the swimmer's rescue if her only danger were that of catching cold, or if she were in danger of drowning, but there was little hope of his saving her and every prospect of being drowned himself; but he would have an obligation to do so if she were in danger of drowning, and his only reason for reluctance was the fear of getting salt water on a new suit.

§ 3. ACT AND CIRCUMSTANCES

We are now in a position to take up the discussion of Circumstances: What things count as circumstances, and how are they related to and distinguished from Acts? In particular, we shall consider those circumstances which enter into the essential constitution of a good or bad deed, and shall attempt to define them in terms of our earlier conclusions.

(i) *Circumstances in general*

Bentham provides a starting-point with the following helpful footnote:

The etymology of the word circumstance is perfectly characteristic of its import: *circum stantia*, things standing around: objects standing round a given object. I forget what mathematician it was that defined God to be a circle, of which the centre is every where, but the circumference no where. In like manner, the field of circumstances, belonging to any act, may be defined a circle, of which the circumference is no where, but of which the act in question is the centre. Now then, as any act may, for the purpose of discourse, be considered as a centre, any other act or object whatsoever may be considered as of the number of those that are standing round it.[1]

Such an account has at least three advantages. First, it allows

[1] p. 77, n. 1.

for the wide diversity of contexts in which it is appropriate to speak of circumstances. Circumstances may be of importance to the appraisal of many other kinds of performance than moral ones: of artistic performances, for instance, as when one recalls the circumstance of Beethoven's having been deaf when he wrote the last Quartets, or of Ronald Knox's having restricted himself to beginning each of eight consecutive verses with the same initial letter when translating an alphabetical psalm; or to athletic appraisals, as when one points out that a sprinter's time was indeed slower than in previous performances, but that he was running into a strong headwind on this occasion; or to any appraisal of an act or an article as conducing to a particular purpose, or overall set of purposes, as when we remark on the high petrol consumption of a motor-car which is in other ways economical, or the possibility of dockside strikes in a country which in other ways promises a good import market. Facts and considerations may also count as relevant circumstances in investigations that are not evaluative, but causal; they may be features of a process or phenomenon which are unusual or puzzling or enlightening, or details about the instruments or materials used, or the procedure followed, or the conditions prevailing, say of temperature, or pressure, or humidity, or the presence or intensity of magnetic or electrical disturbance, or the state of an organism's metabolism. Nor are circumstance-terms restricted to evaluative and causal investigations; they may occur in purely descriptive propositions and passages: embellish a story, add to its explanatory content, convey information about aspects of the narrative that are curious or amusing or poignant.

Second, the lines quoted do justice to the fact that there is often considerable relativity in the application of the terms 'act' and 'circumstances'. Frequently, when discussing the same episode, we may in one context speak of p as the act, and q, r, and s as the circumstances, but in another context speak of q as the act, and p, r, and s as the circumstances.

Gielgud might feel that the satisfaction derived from playing Othello for the first time was heightened by the circumstance of the performance's being at Stratford; but the Stratford Committee might feel that the fact of its being Gielgud's first appearance in the role was a circumstance that enhanced their production.

Third, the passage is easily extended to provide for the feature of non-includedness, which so often marks off 'circumstances' from 'act', and is one aspect of the relativism that exists between them. Suppose again that a given episode comprises the features p, q, r, and s. If p is expressed by an act-term, then q, r, and s will be circumstances to it. But if one uses a single act-term to express p and q, then, once that act-description has been settled, q is not a circumstance of the act, but an element in its definition. Once the appropriate act-description has been settled, circumstances are at least negatively definable as facts or considerations not included in the definition of the act-term employed.

Where moral discourse is specifically in question, these remarks of Bentham suggest a method of picturing the distinction, which we often wish to draw, between *act* and *offence*: the same act may, in different circumstances, constitute different offences, or no offence at all. To accommodate a suggestion of Bentham's own, the act of sexual intercourse may, in different circumstances, constitute a case of adultery, or of rape, or it may constitute an exercise of the rights of marriage; or again, the act of killing a man may, in different circumstances, constitute a case of murder, or of manslaughter, or of justifiable homicide. The model of Bohr's atom suggests itself. First, *this* nucleus when surrounded by *this* number and arrangement of electrons gives us *this* sort of atom; in the same way, *this* act when surrounded or accompanied by *these* circumstances gives us *this* sort of offence. Second, a single word, e.g. 'oxygen-atom', connotes the whole complex of this particular arrangement of constituent nucleus and satellites; and in the same way, a single word, e.g. adultery, connotes the whole complex of this act and these circumstances. Third, without the electrons orbiting around it, the nucleus is not an oxygen-atom; and in the same way, without the necessary circumstances, the act is not the offence in question: e.g. the act of killing a man is not murder if the circumstance of intentionality is lacking, and the act of sexual intercourse is not adultery if neither of the parties is married, or if they are married to each other. Bentham has successfully allowed for the fact that a given circumstance may be internal to the concept of the offence, but external to that of the act under a narrower description.

The spatial metaphor suggested by the etymology of the term *circum stantia*, as it is also by the distinction between what is internal and what external, is therefore quite useful. Occasionally, perhaps, one may wonder a little uneasily whether Bentham has forgotten that it is only a metaphor: acts, he says, are 'objects', and circumstances 'stand around them'; they are 'entities': indeed, they are 'a sort of real archetypal entities'. This uneasiness may be most marked when he is speaking of an offence as constituted out of an act and criminative circumstances; it is almost as if he were conceiving an offence literally as a cluster, a discrete core surrounded by a number of other discrete entities. But the valuable points which Bentham has made may be retained even if the spatial image is left aside, and we speak simply of act-terms and circumstance-terms. A fact or consideration may then feature as a circumstance-term, provided only that it is not an element in the definition of the act-term being employed: thus, the fact that I acted intentionally is a circumstance of my act under the description 'homicide', but not under the description 'murder'. To use a non-spatial metaphor, one might say that a circumstance-term plays a quasi-adverbial role, once the act-description is settled; it modifies the act-term, whose role is quasi-verbal. The circumstance-term is not necessarily, of course, a grammatical adverb: to the statement, 'A did X', it is not restricted to adding information about the verb 'did'; it may qualify or amplify A, or X, and be grammatically adjectival. It is adverbial in the sense that it modifies the force of the act-term; in a proposition submitting an act to moral evaluation, for instance, it may affect our verdict on the agent's *act* by giving us information about him, or about his victim: say, that he was insane, and therefore not guilty; or that it was a very poor person from whom he had stolen, and that his act was therefore worse than had at first appeared. But whatever of metaphors, two things seem clear. First, one cannot lay down two separate lists, one of words and phrases that count always as act-terms, the other of words and phrases that count only as circumstance-terms. Second, circumstances are, however, negatively definable in the sense that, once the act-description has been chosen, they are facts and considerations not included in the definition of the act-term employed.

(ii) *Morally significant circumstances*

Where there is question of circumstances which are relevant to moral evaluation, Bentham discusses those only which affect a wrongful deed, or offence; and he thinks that they may do so by entering into the constitution of the offence, or by modifying it once constituted. He calls the former kind 'criminative circumstances'; since we are interested in good deeds as well as bad, let us call them 'constitutive circumstances'.

These may be defined quite briefly in terms of our earlier discussion of Moral Species. There are certain kinds of acts which constantly recur in recognizable patterns, and are of great importance for human happiness and welfare; we called the terms which denote them 'moral-species-terms'. These terms are commonly capable of fairly precise definition, and I suggest that the facts and considerations which are the elements of such definitions may conveniently be called 'constitutive circumstances'. For instance, it was suggested above that there are four elements in the definition of *theft*: the theft of B's x is ascribed to A if, and only if, (1) A took x; (2) x did not belong to him, but to B; (3) he did not return it to B, but consumed, sold, or destroyed it; (4) B had not given A leave for the action. These four elements, then, would be the constitutive circumstances of the moral-species 'theft', and an inquiry into a charge of theft would be primarily concerned to establish the presence or absence of each of these circumstances.

Let us compare with this Bentham's account. He is pursuing his objective of drawing up a system based on one single, overriding criterion, the Principle of Utility, and is determined to judge the morality of an act solely in the light of its consequences. Accordingly he begins by defining a material, i.e. relevant, circumstance as 'any object whatsoever when it bears a visible relation in point of causality to the consequences'; and it may bear such a relation, he thinks, in four ways. He sets these out and illustrates them in reference to the murder of the Duke of Buckingham by a man called Fenton in 1628. Buckingham was a minister of Charles I, and Fenton was exasperated by his maladministration; he went down from London to Portsmouth, found Buckingham in a group of people, drew a knife, and stabbed him. Now a circumstance may be related to the consequence of an act, says Bentham, (1) in the way of *causation*, when it contributes to the production of the consequence: e.g. Fenton's drawing his knife, going to Portsmouth, becoming angry at Buckingham's maladministration, the maladministration itself; (2) in the way of *derivation*, when it is one of the events produced by the act: e.g. the resulting bloodiness of Fenton's knife; (3) in the way of *collateral connexion*, when the circumstance and consequence in question have nothing to do with each other's production, but are related to a common object which has been concerned in the production of them both: e.g. the finding of Fenton's hat upon the ground where it had fallen 'in the effort', or the finding in the crown of the hat of pieces of paper on which he had written his purpose; (4) in the way of *conjunct influence*, when the circumstance and the act have concurred in producing the consequence: e.g. the situation and conversations of people around Buckingham distracting his attention from danger, together with Fenton's entering the room, jointly contributed to the receiving of the wound. The following footnote is added:

The division may be farther illustrated and confirmed by the more simple and particular case of animal generation. To production corresponds paternity: to derivation, filiation: to collateral connexion, collateral consanguinity; to conjunct influence, marriage and copulation.[1]

In the light of this, Bentham gives the following statement of the role and relationship of act and circumstances in the constitution of an offence:

An act of some sort or other is necessarily included in the notion of every offence. Together with this act, under the notion of the same offence, are included certain circumstances: which circumstances enter into the essence of the offence, contribute by their conjunct influence to the production of its consequences, and in conjunction with the act are brought into view by the name by which it stands distinguished. These we shall have occasion to distinguish hereafter by the name of *criminative* circumstances.[2]

Such an account makes explicitly a distinction for which we noticed earlier that Bentham had implicitly provided: the distinction which we often wish to make between 'act' and 'offence'. One may say that the same act, in different circumstances, constitutes different offences: the act of killing may, in different circumstances, constitute the offence of murder, the offence of manslaughter, or a case of justifiable homicide.

[1] p. 78, n. 1.   [2] p. 80.

But this is a distinction which we do not make quite rigorously: we may also speak of an act of murder, or an act of manslaughter; whereas Bentham would say that an act cannot be an offence unless it is combined with certain circumstances. For his account also involves a rigorous distinction between 'act' and 'circumstances' in the constitution of an offence. If p, q, r, and s are the elements in the definition of the species-term X, my own suggestion is that any of the four may count as a circumstance while one is investigating whether a given individual act may be characterized as X; whereas Bentham would hold that, say, the features p and q belong only to the act, and r and s only to the circumstances. This is a departure from the earlier remarks in which he recognized the relativity of the terms 'act' and 'circumstances', and it does less than justice to the flexibility which they exhibit in ordinary language.

I think that the point is worth pursuing. It might be suspected that this criticism has attributed to Bentham as a formal doctrine what is nothing more than a verbal slip. Let us then consider a later passage where he argues for a strict distinction between 'act' and 'circumstances', at least where voluntary acts are in question:

Now the circumstances of an act are no objects of intention. A man intends the act: and by his intention produces the act: but as to the circumstances, he does not intend *them*: he does not, inasmuch as they are circumstances of it, produce them. . . . Acts, with their consequences, are objects of the will, as well as of the understanding: circumstances, as such, are objects of the understanding only. All he can do with these, as such, is to know or not to know them.[1]

The point is illustrated in another assassination example which Bentham discusses at length: William Tyrrel's shooting and killing King William II with an arrow.[2] Such things as the firing of the arrow, its force and direction, its entering

[1] p. 88.   [2] pp. 85–87, 90–91.

and wounding and killing the King, come under the terms 'act' and 'consequences', for Tyrrel willed and intended, and produced, them. But the King's proximity, or the speed or direction of his approach, could be known, but not produced, by Tyrrel; they were merely circumstances of his act. Since we are concerned only with acts which are voluntary, Bentham appears to say, that only counts as an act which is in the control of the will. Things which are not produced by the will immediately (and so not *part* of one's act) nor subsequently (and so not *consequences* of the act) can be nothing but *circumstances* of the act. For Bentham, then, the phrase 'circumstances beyond my control' would be pleonastic.

In this he appears to have overlooked the great flexibility which circumstance-language exhibits, and to which he had earlier done justice. It is hardly surprising, then, that this stipulation is difficult to square with some of his own terminology and examples. This is particularly true of circumstances which are connected with a given consequence by way of 'causation' and 'derivation'. In the case which he quoted to illustrate these terms, Bentham gave the name 'circumstances' to Fenton's travelling down to Portsmouth, making his way into Buckingham's room, and drawing his knife: all, surely, Fenton's own doing. He also calls a circumstance 'the resulting bloodiness of the knife' after the stabbing; it would be very odd to say that Fenton could only know that, and not produce it.

Furthermore, this restriction is at odds with Bentham's frequent references to 'intentionality', i.e. the fact of an act's being intentional, as a circumstance. It would follow, then, that one might know that one's act was intentional, but could not intend it to be intentional; or, in his own terminology, intentionality would be an object of the understanding, but not of the will. Again, he sometimes refers to motive as a circumstance. He would have to say, then, that one can know one's motive, but not intend it—a little reminiscent, this, of the idea of Ross and Prichard that we cannot produce motives at will. But one sense of the word 'motive' is 'intended consequence'; it would follow, then, that one cannot intend the consequences one intends. Indeed, this passage has the paradoxical implication that 'consequences' are objects of the will, as well as of the understanding; whereas 'intended consequences' are objects of the understanding only.

Apart from these inconsistencies within Bentham's account, such a rigorous limitation on the things which may be called circumstances is hardly borne out by usage. It is quite true that there are some types of circumstance-language for which the restriction holds good. Such phrases as 'the circumstances in which he found himself', and 'the circumstances in which he acted', do indeed commonly refer to facts or features of a situation which the agent himself did not produce and might not be able to control; for instance, we may say of the captain who jettisons cargo when in danger of shipwreck that, given the circumstances in which he had to act, it was the only thing for him to do, and his action was justified: the suggestion being that the circumstances were not of his own making. But a great deal of circumstance-language is subject to no such restriction. We often say, for instance, that the essential malice of an act was mitigated or aggravated by circumstances which accompanied it and which the agent himself produced: that a murder, for example, was accompanied by circumstances of great cruelty. The general point is that it makes perfectly good sense to draw a distinction between circumstances which are, and those which are not, beyond one's control; the distinction is both possible and useful, and commonly invoked in ordinary language.

This rigorous limitation on what may count as act and what as circumstances, then, has influenced Bentham in his analysis of an offence. Two types of element are required for the constitution of an offence, he says: an act, and the appropriate criminative circumstances. They are included together in the definition of the offence, and they combine together to constitute its essence; they are distinct from each other. Such an account leads to some odd conclusions. An act will be bad, or wrongful, only when it is joined with certain features not included in the definition of that act; these other features, the criminative circumstances, are 'essential ingredients of the offence' as much as is the act with which they combine; neither without the other is an offence, as neither an acid-radical nor a base-radical is a salt without the other. No *act*, therefore, is bad, or wrongful. Now such a conclusion is simply not sanctioned by the day-to-day language of morals. We commonly say that robbery, murder, rape, and torture are bad acts; but Bentham must say that they are not acts at all. For him, each of them would be an offence, of which the act is only a part; there could not be a bad act, any more than there can be a saline acid-radical. In other words, no act-term can be the subject of a proposition expressing moral disapproval; or, no term to which an (at least unfavourable) predicate of moral evaluation applies is an act-term. To hold this *ex professo* would be to legislate very boldly indeed against the usage, not only of ordinary English, but also of other languages, both 'ordinary' and philosophical, as far back as Aristotle's πρᾶξις.

Indeed, where one is discussing the circumstances relevant to the moral evaluation of an act, one may feel that Aristotle's τὰ καθ' ἕκαστα ἐν οἷς καὶ περὶ ἃ ἡ πρᾶξις is much closer to our actual usage of the term 'circumstances' than are Bentham's rather strict definitions. Aristotle is considering the effect of ignorance on the voluntariety of an act: general ignorance does not render an act non-voluntary, he says, but particular ignorance may, i.e. ignorance of the particular circumstances of the act, or the things affected by it. The particular facts or features of a performance, he thinks, may be reduced to six headings: (1) the agent: the person who performs the action;

(2) the act itself: what he does; (3) what or whom he is acting upon; (4) the instrument with which he acts; (5) the end or aim or purpose of the act; (6) the manner of acting, e.g. gently or roughly.[1] It looks as if Aristotle may consider that this list is exhaustive; for every possible relevant fact belongs either to the act itself (2) or (3), its efficient cause, whether principal (1) or instrumental (4), its final cause (5), or some aspect of the manner of its performance (6). Aristotle would presumably claim that other heads of circumstances would fall under one or other of his six: e.g. Cicero's *ubi* and *quando* under (6). It is natural to translate ἐν οἷς as 'circumstances', and hence to say that Aristotle counts as circumstances every conceivable feature of the act: for although in line 1 he refers to them all as the particulars ἐν οἷς καὶ περὶ ἃ ἡ πρᾶξις, in lines 16, 19, and 24 he refers to them all simply as the particulars ἐν οἷς ἡ πρᾶξις. This is not a point to press; one does not wish to introduce the appearance of rigour just at the moment when one is appealing for flexibility. But it is quite compatible with such an appeal to suggest that if each of the six headings were to be placed either under ἐν οἷς or under περὶ ἅ, then (2), τί, the act itself, would naturally fall under ἐν οἷς; that is, Aristotle is not advocating any rigorous distinction between τί and ἐν οἷς ἡ πρᾶξις: just as, I would suggest, there is no general, rigorous distinction to be drawn between 'act' and 'circumstances'.

For against any rather doctrinaire definitions such as Bentham's, I want to suggest that the term 'circumstances' is very loosely defined indeed; that there is no general rule for deciding what sort of things are circumstances, and what sort are acts; that while we are arriving at the appropriate characterization of, or judgement on, an act, any relevant fact may be mentioned as a circumstance. 'Circumstances' is therefore not a technical term referring to some precisely defined element in the human performance, but a useful word for

[1] *Eth. Nic.*, 1111ᵃ 1–24.

referring to any fact or group of facts that contributes to our reaching a satisfactory description, characterization, or appraisal of a person's act. When we inquire about, or discuss, 'the circumstances', or say that we are diffident about passing judgement on an act until we know 'all the circumstances', we usually mean simply 'all the relevant facts of the case'. We do not mean, 'I know what the *act* was; now tell me the circumstances'; some of the circumstances will probably turn out to be elements in the definition of the term which is ultimately used to characterize the act. There are no grounds for thinking that certain terms may refer only to acts, and others only to circumstances, as some terms apply only to physical properties and others only to chemical ones; a dictionary could not, as well as putting *v.* or *adv.* after a word to indicate whether it was a verb or an adverb, also put *a.* or *c.* after it to indicate whether it was an act-term or a circumstance-term. We may say that an act of X is a case of Y; but we will often then be able to attribute indifferently to the agent an act of X *or* an act of Y. Bentham calls beating a man an act, and that is perfectly proper; but there is nothing improper in our also calling it, given the appropriate circumstances, an act of cruelty, or an act of revenge.

Let us now briefly summarize our principal conclusions concerning the ways in which 'act' and 'consequences', and 'act' and 'circumstances', are mutually related and distinguished. In each case we found that there is considerable flexibility in the appropriate use of these terms, and considerable relativity between each pair. One cannot lay down what properties are to determine whether a given word is an act-term, a circumstance-term, or a consequence-term; we found that Bentham, when he attempted to do so, was led to conclusions which were inconsistent with other things he had written, and did violence to ordinary usage. One cannot draw up three separate lists of words so that those in the first may serve only as act-terms, those in the second only as

circumstance-terms, and those in the third only as conse-
quence-terms.

The mutual relativity of 'act' and 'consequences' is seen
in this, that some possible descriptions of the act are what
we should call descriptions of its consequences if we adopted
a term of narrower connotation as the description of the act
itself. However, this relativity is not unlimited. On the one
hand, we argued against Austin that there is no justification
for demanding a fixed act/consequences distinction between
the muscular movements involved in a given performance
and the later elements in it: that many of the things which
chronologically succeed the muscular movements are not
consequences of them, but equally with them part of the
act; and we urged that we simply adopt the ordinary way of,
and terms for, speaking about acts. On the other hand, we
found that ordinary usage insists that there are cases in which
an act/consequence distinction *must* be drawn at a certain
point. There are some kinds of act—'moral species'—so
significant for human living that they seem to complete a
chain; they are an act, not just part of an act; what follows
them is a consequence of that act, not just a later stage of it.
Whenever the elements of their definition are verified, they
warrant explicit mention in a separate act-description.

The distinction between 'act' and 'circumstances' is even
more loosely defined. We argued against Bentham that there
is no justification for demanding a hard and fast act/circum-
stances distinction between those factors which are and are
not in the control of the agent; when we are seeking to characterize or evaluate a human performance, any relevant fact
or consideration may be counted among the circumstances.
The phrase 'constitutive circumstances' applies to any of the
'essential ingredients of an offence' or good deed; for we
held against Bentham that one cannot divide the elements
in a species-definition into those which belong to the act and
those which belong to the circumstances: all of them are

constitutive circumstances, and all of them belong to the act-definition. Only two restrictions were found to be necessary: phrases such as 'the circumstances in which he acted' refer to features of the situation not included in the act-description employed; and, *after* an act-description has been chosen, the term 'circumstances' will apply only to facts and considerations not included in its definition. Given these two exceptions, Bentham's first thoughts seem best: as any act may, for the purpose of discourse, be considered a centre, any other act or object may be considered as of the number of those that are standing around it, i.e. its *circum stantia*.

2

THE CLASSIFICATION OF CIRCUMSTANCES

So far we have investigated, as Bentham says, 'the act itself, and the general assemblage of the circumstances with which it may have been accompanied'; and we have paid attention to one particular type of circumstances that affect the act's morality. Next, we must consider the classification of circumstances according to their bearing on the moral evaluation of an act. We shall first consider Bentham's classification and then, in the light of what emerges, suggest an alternative arrangement.

§ I. BENTHAM'S ARRANGEMENT

Bentham's method of classifying morally relevant circumstances is best seen in the passage whose first part we have already considered:

An act of some sort or other is necessarily included in the notion of every offence. Together with this act, under the notion of the same offence, are included certain circumstances: which circumstances enter into the essence of the offence, contribute by their conjunct influence to the production of its consequences, and in conjunction with the act are brought into view by the name by which it stands distinguished. These we shall have occasion to distinguish hereafter by the name of *criminative* circumstances. Other circumstances again entering into combination with the act and the former set of circumstances, are productive of still farther consequences. These additional consequences, if they are of beneficial kind, bestow, according to the value they bear in that capacity, upon the circumstances to which they owe their birth, the appellation of *exculpative* or *extenuative* circumstances: if of the mischievous kind, they bestow on them the appellation of *aggravative* circumstances.[1]

[1] p. 80.

Exculpative, extenuative, and aggravative circumstances are said a little later to *modify* the offence once constituted, and they are sometimes called 'accidental'; and in several places criminative circumstances are called 'essential'.

It will be noticed that in offering this account Bentham is strictly faithful to his original Utilitarian programme, classifying circumstances in reference to consequences. One need not subscribe to that programme to agree that the first thing is to distinguish between circumstances according as they make a difference in kind or a difference in degree to the morality of the act on which they bear: this Bentham does by distinguishing first between Criminative or essential circumstances on the one hand, and Modifying or accidental circumstances on the other. On six other scores, however, the arrangement seems less happy.

1. Bentham provides only for those circumstances which affect the moral value of *bad* acts, or offences; but an adequate account should also deal with their bearing on *good* acts. To this he would probably reply that he is interested in drawing up a basis for a criminal code, and hence that it is only offences with whose structure and division he is concerned. But the title of his book promises an introduction to the principles of morals as well as legislation, and morals are concerned with good acts as well as bad; Chapter 1 proposes a thorough-going application of the Principle of Utility because it is the sole test of right and wrong, not just of wrong; Chapter 7, in which circumstances are divided and classified, is entitled 'Of Human Actions in General', not just 'Of Wrongful Actions'; and at the end of Chapter 9 Bentham declares that the definitions and distinctions which he has made are of great importance 'as well to moral discourse as to legislative practice', and that they help to determine the good as well as the bad consequences of an act. To restrict Constitutive Circumstances (as we called them in Chapter 1) to criminative ones seems therefore to neglect half of the

question. Nor is it enough to classify Modifying Circumstances according as they cancel, mitigate, or aggravate the guilt of a bad act: one also needs to say how they affect the worth of a good one.

2. Even where bad acts are alone in question there are three ways in which circumstances may affect the morality of an act *in kind*. First, a circumstance may be a necessary element in the definition of a given moral species: as the fact that the thing taken belongs to another person is a necessary element in the definition of theft. Second, a circumstance may cause an act which is an instance of the species of wrongdoing X to be also, at the same time, an instance of another species Y: for example, a statement which is a lie may also be perjury, because of the fact that it is made under oath. Third, a circumstance may cause an act, which without that circumstance would have been an instance of the species of wrongdoing X, not to be a case of X but an instance of species Y: for instance, to have sexual intercourse with another man's wife would normally be adultery; but if it be done forcefully and against her will, it is not adultery, but rape.

Now Bentham speaks of criminative circumstances as producing a certain species of offence. If by this he means the first of the three ways we have distinguished, then he appears to have neglected the other two; if he means to embrace all three, it seems to be a defect that he has not distinguished them out.

3. There are difficulties, apart from classificatory ones, in speaking of Exculpative Circumstances as modifying an offence once constituted. For one thing, the examples of Exculpative Circumstances most frequently given by Bentham are the absence of the necessary intention of consequences or consciousness of circumstances. Now exculpative circumstances are given as a subdivision of Modifying Circumstances, which 'enter into combination' with the

offence once constituted; and it seems strange to speak of the absence of something as entering into combination with something else. Furthermore, the presence of the necessary intention and consciousness are listed among the essential ingredients in the composition of the offence; yet exculpative circumstances, which enter into combination with the offence only when it is constituted, include the absence of the necessary intentionality and consciousness. So an offence is constituted because the essential ingredients p, q, and r are present, and at the same time modified because r is absent.

4. Bentham divides circumstances which modify an offence into (a) exculpative and extenuative; and (b) aggravative. But surely it is 'extenuative' and 'aggravative' which are logically akin; extenuative and aggravative circumstances affect the moral value of an act quantitatively, but exculpative circumstances affect it qualitatively. An exculpative circumstance such as physical incapacity to control one's actions is not a mere afterthought which leads us to add a brief rider to our verdict on the act which it concerns; it belongs with considerations which make a difference in kind, not merely a difference in degree, to our estimate.

In Bentham's own terms, the primary distinction is between those morally relevant circumstances which are criminative or essential, and those which are modifying or accidental. Now exculpative circumstances are on a logical par with the criminative, for the presence of the former has the same effect as, and is often identical with, the latter. Hence exculpative circumstances belong with the essential, and extenuative and aggravative circumstances together belong with the accidental. For Bentham, exculpation commonly arises from the absence of a criminative circumstance; how could the absence of something accidental make an essential difference?

5. But do exculpative circumstances make an essential difference? I suggest that there is an ambiguity in this term

'essential'. It was just suggested that a circumstance such as physical incapacity is not a mere afterthought which modifies the moral verdict on an act accidentally; but then, neither does it serve to identify the act as an instance of this or that moral species; rather, it concerns the conditions which must be fulfilled before there can be a morally responsible act at all, of any species. I propose therefore, in § 2 of this chapter, to distinguish between those circumstances which affect the sheer *existence* of a morally evaluable act, and those which affect the particular moral *species* to which the act belongs, once given that it is amenable to moral appraisal at all.

There is a corresponding ambiguity in the term 'criminative circumstances'. Consider, for instance, the following:

The presence of intention with regard to such or such a consequence, and of consciousness with regard to such or such a circumstance, of the act, will form so many criminative circumstances, or essential ingredients in the composition of this or that offence.[1]

Now the phrase 'essential ingredients in the composition of this or that offence' would seem to apply to the elements logically necessary according to the definition of a particular offence, as is the fact that a person was speaking under oath, in perjury, or the fact that at least one party was married, in adultery. But it is very rarely that this applies to the circumstances of intentionality and consciousness; intentionality is part of the definition of murder, and perhaps also of mayhem, but it is hard to think of many other examples. Intentionality and consciousness seem rather to be connected with the conditions necessary for a person's being guilty of any offence at all, as is the physical capacity to perform or refrain from the act in question. We must examine that connexion in Chapter 3.

[1] p. 96.

6. Finally, Bentham's 'Exculpative Circumstances' seems to be a profoundly ambiguous term, running together two kinds of morally relevant circumstances which should be kept distinct: for some circumstances exculpate by way of *justification*, and others by way of *excuse*. The distinction is implicitly recognized by Bentham when he says that a worthy motive does not render an act of homicide 'innocent', and 'still less beneficial', i.e. good.[1] To say that an act which in normal circumstances would be wicked is by some special circumstance rendered good, would be to say that that circumstance justified it; to say merely that it is rendered innocent is to say rather that, though the act is still disapproved of as wrongful, the agent is not to be blamed for it, and that the circumstance excuses it, or him. A somewhat similar distinction is recognized by Bentham explicitly, at least for legal contexts, in his book *The Limits of Jurisprudence Defined*.[2] He there distinguishes between justificative or exculpative circumstances on the one hand, and exemptive circumstances on the other. The latter, he says, 'take an act out of the case in which it is thought proper to punish it, without taking it out of the case in which it is wished it were not done'. This is rather like an excusing circumstance. A person may be *excused* for having killed, on the score of insanity; but this does not *justify* the killing: it remains 'a case in which it is wished it were not done'. On the other hand, says Bentham, a justificative or exculpative circumstance 'has the effect of taking the act in some particular case or other out of the general case in which the performance or non-performance of it is an offence'. This is what is called more commonly a justifying circumstance. A person may be justified for killing in necessary self-defence; one wishes, indeed, that the need had not arisen, but given that it did, one does not 'wish that it were not done'.

However, this distinction of Bentham's is not quite the

---

[1] p. 165, n. 1. [2] (New York, 1945), pp. 215 and 236.

same as the distinction we make between excuse and justification. He writes:

> The principal law, and the punitory law which is subsidiary to it, are two essentially distinct laws: exculpative provisions then are qualifications to the principal: exemptive ones, to the punitory. . . . Exemptive circumstances are circumstances which limit the application of punishment without limiting the description of the offence. . . . The connection between delinquency and the demand for punishment, however close, is not inseparable: there are cases in which, though guilt in the highest degree be indubitable, yet punishment would be improper.

Bentham's exemptive circumstance is therefore not excusing: for an excusing circumstance means that, for some reason or other, guilt is not present. What these two kinds of circumstance have in common, however, in contrast to justifying circumstances, is that they do not alter the appropriate description of the act. On the other hand, what excusing and justifying circumstances have in common, in contrast to Bentham's exemptive circumstances, is that they involve the absence of guilt, or fault; Bentham could claim good etymological warrant for putting them together under the rubric 'exculpative'. But let us see a little more closely how they are distinct.

The term 'justify' may be applied to a decision, a belief, a practice, and a rule, as well as to an act. In each of these cases it will often be used without moral significance. A politician's decision to base his campaign on a new policy, a general's decision to attack without air-support, a cricket captain's decision to send in his opponents after he has won the toss may each be 'justified in the event', i.e. vindicated or warranted by the result; a scientist's belief in a new theory, or a mother's belief in the innocence of her son despite the verdict of a court, may be justified by subsequent evidence; a practice which displeases the fastidious few may be justified because it pleases the more lusty majority, as seems to have been the case with some of the noisier customs at Elsinore; rules about traffic, or games, or the 'correct' fingering for typing, may be tiresome in the short run, but justified by their long-range advantages; and of course an *act* may be justified in many senses other than the moral, particularly in some of the senses just noted—technically, militarily, economically, politically. It will be noticed that to say that a decision, belief, practice, rule, or act was justified is usually to imply that one's first reaction was to say that there was something wrong with it, though subsequently (on learning the circumstances, or in the light of the consequences) to decide, agree, or admit that it was right: we say that something is justified only when we think, or expect that someone will think, that it needs justification. These two features are present in the normal use of the term 'justification' in moral contexts, where it is used particularly of practices and acts, and to some extent of rules. For instance, the institution of punishment needs justification, since it involves the deliberate infliction of suffering or deprivation on a human being, though we may be persuaded that it is right on retributive, deterrent, or reformative grounds. To speak of justifying moral rules is perhaps peculiar to moral philosophers: for instance, a champion of Restricted Utilitarianism says that 'we justify particular actions by reference to general rules, and we justify the rules by reference to the Principle of Utility'; but ordinary usage does not ask that the rules against murder, torture, or lying be 'justified', for it is not one's first reaction to feel that such rules are wrong. Finally, in a moral context, we may say that an *act* is justified. To say that an act is justified by some special circumstance is to say that (1) were that circumstance not present it would have been a wrongful act: thus we may speak of justifiable homicide, but not of justifiable life-saving; and (2) given all the circumstances, it was a good act, or 'the right thing to do'.

In a moral context, therefore, where it is an act which is

under discussion, we may distinguish the terms 'justify', 'excuse', 'pardon', and 'condone'. If an act is justified, the agent is responsible for it, but the act is, in the circumstances, not wrong. If it is excused, the act is a wrongful one, but the agent is, because of some special circumstances, not responsible for it, and hence not guilty. If it is pardoned, there is both wrongfulness and responsibility, and hence guilt, but the offended person or the competent authority decides not to hold its guilt against the agent, and to act as if it had not happened. If it is condoned, there is both wrongfulness and responsibility, but some relevant person acquiesces in the act and approves, or at least refrains from expressing disapproval, of the agent's performing it. This perhaps is why 'condone' is commonly used of a third party: one may say that A is condoning B's misdeeds, for instance that Chamberlain condoned Hitler's seizing Czechoslovakia; but one does not say '*I* condone B's misdeeds', for that would be to say that one approves of something which one believes to be wrong; rather, one protests that, in the circumstances, B's act is justified. One may say, 'I condoned B's misdeeds', but only in retrospective self-accusation.

These terms are not all perfectly distinct, but tend to shade off one into the other. This is particularly true of the distinction with which we are at present concerned, that between 'justify' and 'excuse'. The late Professor J. L. Austin wondered, for instance, about the exact status of the plea of provocation: does it mean that the provocation roused a violent impulse or passion in the agent, who was therefore not entirely responsible for his act (excuse)? Or is it that, having suffered an injury, he was entitled to retaliate (justification)?[1] However, as Austin remarked, the existence of such borderline cases cannot make us doubt that the two pleas are in principle distinct. The distinction is fairly well

[1] 'A Plea for Excuses', *Proceedings of the Aristotelian Society*, 1956–7, p. 3.

indicated by the derivation of the two words; later in the same paper Austin pointed out that a word hardly ever entirely shakes off its origin and root, and that, when inquiring into the logic of philosophically important terms, it is often instructive to have an eye for their 'trailing clouds of etymology'; and our present question provides a case in point. The effect of a *justifying* circumstance is to *justum facere* an (otherwise wrongful) act, so that it becomes good, or at least permissible: lawful. We regret that the circumstance has arisen but, given that it has, we feel that the agent acted rightly, or 'within his rights', and we approve of his act; for instance if, in legitimate self-defence, A wounds his assailant B, we regret that the necessity arose but, since it did, we feel that A was entitled to act as he did. The effect of an *excusing* circumstance is to put the wrongful act *ex causa*, outside the court of moral verdict at all. We still disapprove of the act, and consider it unwarranted; we do not think that the agent was entitled to do it, but simply recognize that some condition necessary for personal responsibility was lacking in him: for instance if A, through insanity, attacks and wounds B, we do not think that A's act was warranted, or that he had any right to perform it, but simply that he was not responsible for the act, and so not to be blamed. When a merely excusing circumstance is present, then, the act remains objectively immoral, but the agent is not guilty, because not responsible; whereas when a justifying circumstance is present, the agent is perfectly responsible, but his act is rendered objectively lawful.

How does a justifying circumstance work? It is natural to look for an answer in terms of the moral-species terminology which we accommodated from Bentham in Chapter 1, and this certainly seems a convenient way of accounting for two kinds of justifying circumstance. First, there is the type of case in which the act without the justifying circumstance is an instance of a species to which one of the dyslogistic predicates of moral evaluation applies, but is transformed by its presence into an instance of a species to which one of the commendatory predicates applies. For instance, for A to cut off B's leg would, justifying circumstances apart, be an act of mayhem; but given that A is a surgeon and that the leg is gangrenous, it becomes an act of charity. In some respects this is similar to those cases in which a circumstance renders an act, which without that circumstance would be an instance of the offence-species X, an instance of the offence-species Y: as, for example, an act which would otherwise be a case of adultery is rendered, by the circumstance of the woman's unwillingness, a case of rape. The presence of this first type of circumstance is like that in that it effects a change of species; but it is unlike it in that it does a great deal more. Not only does it change the species; it also changes the genus, to use Bentham's term: and not only from one *genus infimum*, as he calls them, to another, but also from one *genus supremum* to another: changes it, namely, from membership of a species which belongs to the *genus supremum* 'offence' or 'wrong-doing', to a species of the *genus supremum* 'virtuous act'.

However, it is not necessary that a justifying circumstance transform the (otherwise wrongful) act into a virtuous or meritorious one. It is sufficient that the act be rendered objectively permissible, one which the agent is entitled to perform; it need not be the sort of act which he is praised for performing. A second, and perhaps more common, source of justification, then, is not the presence of some additional circumstance with the resulting production of a case of a new species, but the absence of one of the elements in an offence-species-definition. In such cases, an instance of the offence X is present when the features p, q, r, and s are present; and the act in question is justified because, although, p, q, and r are present, s is not. For instance, we have suggested that the conditions of the *theft* of B's X being attributed to A are (1) A took X; (2) X did not belong to A, but to B; (3) A did not return it to B, but consumed, sold, or destroyed it; and (4) B had not given A leave for his action. A's taking and using B's palette, or petrol, or purse, ceases therefore to be theft, and is justified, by the fact that B had given him leave: the fourth element in the definition is lacking. There is nothing meritorious about using a man's petrol; it is enough for justification that A was entitled to act as he did. A more controversial case involves the suggestion that the definition of 'lie' is fulfilled only when listeners are likely to take the speaker seriously: it is not a lie when an actor says, 'The potent poison quite o'ercrows my spirit', even though it is not true. Now take the case of a man in one of the new countries seeking their independence; he belongs to a party which is determined to break the constitutional link with the colonial power. He is elected as leader of the Government, but before he can take office he must take the prescribed pledge to uphold the Constitution; he therefore openly announces that he will pronounce the prescribed formula, but without any internal assent to what he says: he will simply make the noises that the law requires. No doubt some people will say that this would be an immoral step, because 'it is always wrong to tell a lie'; and his supporters will probably make two sorts of reply. Some may say, 'That is true as a general rule; but this is obviously an exception to the rule.' Others, however, may say, 'I agree; but in these circumstances you cannot call it a lie. For a statement to be characterized as a lie, it is necessary that hearers should have reason to think that the speaker means what he says. Where there can be no deception, there is no lie.' Each of these replies will be urged as a justification in the sense that, in the circumstances, the proposed utterance is permissible.

Of course, the absence of an element in the species-definition is not a sufficient condition for justification; it may simply mean that the act becomes an instance of some other offence-species. Killing may cease to be murder because the element of intentionality is absent, but be a case of man-slaughter because of the presence of negligence.

But then, neither is the absence of an element in the species-definition a necessary condition for justification: as we see in the third way that it occurs. A rule of the form 'X is wrong' is often understood as being subject to certain exceptions; when they arise it is agreed that X is justified. For instance, an act of X may be justified when the reason why X is normally held to be wrong would on this occasion be frustrated if X were not done: when, for example, to fulfil a promise would do greater harm to the promisee than would breaking it, or to keep a secret would do more harm to the person who confided it than would revealing it. Again, justification may arise from the urgent personal need of oneself or another. This will often justify, for example, using or damaging another person's property: for instance, A's giving B's brandy to C who is suffering a heart-attack, or a fireman's smashing a door to rescue someone trapped in a burning building, or A's driving into B's parked car, because that is the only way to avoid knocking down a pedestrian. The rule 'Killing is wrong' is an important example of rules, of the form 'X is wrong' being subject to certain recognized exceptions; it does not apply (most people would say) to killing in self-defence, legitimate warfare, or the execution of a condemned criminal. Now when one says that A's killing B in self-defence was justified, one does not mean that the definition of killing was not fulfilled, but that in the circumstances A was entitled to kill; it was 'justifiable homicide'. In cases of this third kind, then, the act continues to be X, but ceases to be wrong; the justifying-circumstance affects, not the species-description of the act, but the predicate of its moral evaluation.

To sum up, then, there are three possible defences against the charge 'A did ϕ, which is an instance of the species X; and it is wrong to do X'. The first, of course, is to deny that A did

ϕ. The second is to admit that A did ϕ, and that ϕ is an instance of X, and therefore wrong; but to argue that some element necessary for morally responsible action was absent in A, and hence that he was not to blame. This is defence by way of excuse, and the fact or consideration on which it is based is an *excusing* circumstance. The third is to admit that A did ϕ, that he was fully responsible for his action, and that in normal circumstances ϕ would be wrong; but to argue that, because of some particular circumstance C, ϕ is either good or at least permissible. This is defence by way of justification, and C is a *justifying* circumstance; and there are three possible ways of putting this defence.

(*a*) It is true that, without C, ϕ would be an instance of X, and therefore wrong; but given C, ϕ is an instance of the species Y, and therefore good.

(*b*) It is true that, without C, ϕ would be an instance of X, and therefore wrong; but given C, ϕ does not fulfil the species definition X, and is permissible.

(*c*) It is true that ϕ is an instance of X; but given C, this is one of the recognized exceptions to the rule 'X is wrong', and ϕ is good or at least permissible.

An excusing circumstance, therefore, primarily affects the agent; a justifying circumstance primarily affects the act: its species-description, or its moral appraisal. Both these kinds of circumstance, then, may indeed be gathered under Bentham's heading 'exculpative', for each of them renders *ex culpa* an agent who would otherwise be at fault; but the single rubric fails to show that they do so in very different ways.

§ 2. AN ALTERNATIVE ARRANGEMENT

A number of points have thus emerged in the course of discussing Bentham's arrangement of circumstances according to their bearing on the moral evaluation of an act. Let us now attempt to incorporate these points in a suggested alternative classification.

First, there are circumstances which concern the conditions which must be present in the agent if his act is to be brought to the bar of moral appraisal at all. Second, given these conditions, there are circumstances which affect the moral species to which the act belongs. It is to these species that the ordinary predicates of moral evaluation apply, and according to the species to which an act is found to belong it is judged good or bad, right or wrong. Third, given that essential verdict, other circumstances may yet affect the degree of goodness or badness that the act is judged to have. Let us label these three classes of circumstances as, respecttively, 'Qualifying'; 'Specifying'; and 'Quantifying'.

Three remarks need to be made about these labels. First, we are classifying circumstances according to the effect that they have on the moral verdict passed on the act, and not on the way that they work. If the latter were in question, it would be natural to distinguish first between those circumstances which affect the agent and those which affect the act. But for our purpose that would lead to overlapping. Some circumstances which affect the agent may simply, say, extenuate the demand for punishment due to the act, while others lead us to say that what he did was not an act at all, in the sense relevant to morals. Second, it is worth remarking that the 'trailing clouds of etymology' would be misleading with regard to the term 'qualifying'. Here, as commonly in English, it does not refer to circumstances which can *qualem facere* the act, make it of this or that species or kind; it is used in the sense that we speak of the 'qualifying conditions' for admission to a university: almost as an opposite of 'disqualifying'. The participles or adjectives 'qualifying' and 'quantifying' are not here related as are the nouns 'quality' and 'quantity'. Third, the term 'quantifying' is not used here in the sense in which it is used in formal logic; it is simply a convenient term to describe circumstances which make a difference in degree to an act's moral worth, as distinct from a difference in kind.

(i) *Qualifying circumstances*

It was remarked earlier in this chapter that a circumstance such as the physical incapacity to control one's actions is not a mere afterthought which leads us to add a brief rider to our verdict on the act which it concerns: it bears on one of the conditions which must be present in the agent if his act is to be susceptible of moral evaluation at all. We may find a parallel in the non-moral sphere by adapting a remark of Rawls: No matter what a person did, he would not be spoken of as 'serving a double-fault', or 'losing the point', unless he was actually playing a game of tennis. He may perform exactly the same movements and produce the same visible effects as would warrant those descriptions were a game in progress; but if it is not—say, because he is 'knocking up', or coaching a pupil—then the conditions necessary for the application of such terms are simply not present. Now similarly, no matter what a person does, he cannot be spoken of as 'committing a moral offence', or 'being morally at fault', unless certain conditions are realized in him. He may go through the very same movements, and produce the very same effects, as would warrant those ascriptions if the conditions were fulfilled; but if they are not, then his act—or, perhaps more accurately, he—simply does not qualify as a candidate for moral praise or blame, approval or disapproval.

The conditions in question are the conditions necessary for moral responsibility, and are here called 'Qualifying Circumstances'; and with these we may bracket 'Disqualifying Circumstances'. A fact or consideration may be called a qualifying circumstance if it assures us that some condition necessary for moral responsibility is fulfilled, or dispels the suspicion that it is not; it may be called a disqualifying circumstance if it is incompatible with the fulfilment of such a condition. Where an otherwise blameworthy act is in question, we have called such disqualifying factors 'Excusing Circumstances'; these include physical incapacity, insanity and its temporary equivalents, duress, and sometimes ignorance, error, inadvertence, and the absence of intention, as we shall discuss in Chapter 3: in general, whatever, at the relevant time, puts the avoidance of a forbidden act, or the performance of an obligatory one, outside the agent's control. Where an otherwise praiseworthy act is in question, we may call such disqualifying factors 'Disentitling Circumstances'; we shall find in the next chapter that good and bad acts are asymmetrical with regard to some of the conditions for their being held to the credit or discredit of the person who performs them, the requirements of Consciousness, Intentionality, and Foresight of Consequences being stricter for laying a good act to his credit than for blaming him for a bad one.

(ii) *Specifying circumstances*

Bentham made a detailed study of offences only, and divided them into so many 'species'; since we are concerned with good acts as well as bad, we extended his term to 'moral species'. He gave the title 'Criminative Circumstances' to the essential ingredients in the composition of this or that offence; so for the corresponding items in species, whether good or bad, the term 'Specifying Circumstances' suggests itself.

We have had occasion to remark on the fact that when one sets about the moral evaluation of an act one does not begin each time from first principles, but seeks to identify it as an instance of some kind, or species. Moral discourse has coined for itself an extensive vocabulary of species-terms, with each of which it associates one of the general predicates of moral evaluation: good or bad, right or wrong, and so on. Most species-terms are susceptible of fairly precise definition, and it is the elements in each such definition which are here called 'Specifying Circumstances'. Several sub-classes may be distinguished.

(*a*) First, there are facts and considerations whose presence is necessary to *constitute* an act as an instance of a given species, or whose absence is sufficient to show that it is not: for instance, intentionality, for murder: or the fact that at least one of the parties is married, for adultery. Under this heading come justifying circumstances of the second type: those, namely, in which an instance of the offence-species X is present when, and only when, the features *p*, *q*, *r*, and *s* are present, and some circumstance shows that the act is justified because, although *p*, *q*, and *r* are present, *s* is not.

(*b*) A circumstance may *change* an act, which without it would be an instance of species X, into an act of species Y. Four types of case are possible. (i) X and Y may both be wrongful, i.e. offence-species. For example, an act which would otherwise be a case of adultery is changed, by the fact of the woman's unwillingness, into a case of rape; or an act which would otherwise be a case of murder may be changed, by the fact of unintentionality through negligence, into a case of manslaughter. (ii) X and Y may both be good: for instance, the circumstance of blood-relationship may change an act of charity into an act of piety. (iii) X may be good but Y wrongful; for example, an act of charity—say, making a donation to a public hospital—may become an act of injustice, when the donor owes the money to a creditor, or will be led to neglect the needs of his family. (iv) X may be wrongful but Y good. This was the case with justifying circumstances of the first type; in the example suggested, an act of mayhem was changed into an act of charity.

(*c*) A circumstance may cause an act to belong to an *additional* species. For instance, a lie may also be perjury because it is spoken on oath, or an act of adultery become also an act of incest because the parties are related by blood. This type of case differs from those noted under (*b*) in that the act belongs to two species at once: committing perjury is also telling a lie, but an act of manslaughter is not murder.

(*d*) A problem is presented by justifying circumstances of the third type: those, namely, that show that the act, though being indeed an instance of the species X, falls under one of the recognized exceptions to the rule that cases of X are wrong. They do not belong under the heading 'Qualifying Circumstances', for they have nothing to do with the agent's responsibility for his act; and they do not belong to 'Quantifying Circumstances', for they make a difference in kind, not just in degree, to the morality of the act which they affect. But perhaps it is not altogether Procrustean to include them among Specifying Circumstances. It is true that they do not affect the characterization of the act as an instance of the species X; but they do serve to locate it in a particular segment of the species, members of which are not subject to the unfavourable verdict that other instances of the species incur.

(iii) *Quantifying circumstances*

Finally, given that the essential verdict of good, or bad, has been passed on a person's act, other circumstances may affect the degree of goodness or badness the act is judged to have. Again, four sub-classes may be distinguished. The first two concern wrongful acts, the second two good ones.

(*a*) *Extenuating* Circumstances mitigate the unfavourable verdict passed on a bad act. This may arise either by way of (i) partial excuse, especially by way of what lawyers call 'diminished responsibility': for instance, culpable ignorance, unintentionality with negligence, fear of financial loss, failure to foresee consequences, some degree of intoxication, or passionate emotion, may not destroy responsibility, but they may lessen it, and hence lessen the wickedness present in performing a wrongful act; or by way of (ii) partial justification, of the third type: that is when, roughly speaking, the act would be justified by a proportionately serious reason and there is some, but not sufficient, reason present: when, for instance, a person uses more violence than is necessary in defending himself, or more violence than is reasonable in defending his property: it is wrong of him to use such violence, but not *so* wrong as if he did the same thing without any provocation or reason.

(*b*) *Aggravating* Circumstances make an already wrongful act even more reprehensible, and may arise from many sources; to give a few examples, they may concern (i) the agent: e.g. that, being in a position of trust, he has been guilty of theft or treason; (ii) the person wronged: e.g. that he is a cripple, in a case of assault, or a poor man, in a case of theft; (iii) the relation between the agent and the person wronged: e.g. that the victim is a parent, or a benefactor; (iv) the object of the act: e.g. that the thing stolen was irreplaceable, and destroyed; or that it was stolen from a grave; (v) the mode of acting: e.g. that murder was done in a way that caused great suffering as well as death.

(*c*) *Enhancing* Circumstances increase the worth of a good act, and may arise from corresponding sources. They may concern (i) the agent: e.g. that the person who undertakes a menial and arduous service is a man of some distinction, or in poor health, or grieved by recent bereavement; a research-worker knows with great clarity the sort of suffering involved if he offers himself for some experiment; (ii) the other party: e.g. that he is unattractive by reason of a surly temperament or a disfiguring disease; (iii) the relation between the agent and the beneficiary: e.g. that the latter wronged the former in the past, or that they belong to rival or enemy groups or nations; (iv) the foreseen by-products or side-effects of the act: e.g. that an act of kindness will involve the agent in loss of a business opportunity or in suspicion of being 'soft' on an enemy nation or doctrine; (v) the mode of acting: e.g. that an act of charity was performed with sensitive care for the pride, dignity, and self-respect of the beneficiary, or promptly and with cheerfulness, giving the impression of being glad to do it.

(*d*) Finally, there are circumstances which *detract from* the worth of a good act. Many of the circumstances which partially excuse the agent of a wrongful act may partially disentitle the agent of a good one, though here again the asymmetry between good and bad acts prevents a strict correspondence; at least we may say that of two men who perform the same deed, that one is less to be commended who acts with less awareness of the likely inconveniences or damages involved, and on impulse rather than after deliberation. The worth of an act may often be diminished by the way it is done: reluctantly, or grudgingly, or condescendingly, or in a way that wounds a beneficiary's pride while alleviating his need. There seems to be nothing in the case of good acts which exactly corresponds to partially justifying circumstances for bad. The nearest equivalent is an unworthy motive; but that is hardly a circumstance, and must be left to Part II.

3

INTENTIONALITY AND CONSCIOUSNESS

THE third and fourth 'articles' which Bentham holds must be considered in the evaluation of any 'transaction' are Intentionality and Consciousness. We have seen that the number of morally relevant circumstances is legion, but these are the only two that he singles out for extended study. To each of them he devotes a whole chapter; and the choice is not surprising. 'The metaphysics of the Stone Age' has embedded in our language the notion that these two points are of peculiar importance in the appraisal of action; we have, 'He did it unintentionally, or unconsciously', 'He omitted it unwittingly': but not, 'He did it insanely', or 'He omitted it incapacitatedly'. I therefore propose to follow Bentham in his choice, though confining myself to one only of several questions he broaches: Are Intentionality and Consciousness necessary Qualifying Circumstances? That is, if either of these is absent, is the agent *ipso facto* to be held not responsible for his act? We shall discuss, first, whether the absence of one of them excuses him from blame for a bad act, and second, whether it disentitles him to the credit of a good one.

§ I. BEARING ON BAD ACTS

Following Bentham's order we shall take Intentionality first and Consciousness second; the discussions will call for a consideration of Negligence under a separate heading.

(i) *Intentionality*

In the chapter 'Cases Unmeet for Punishment', Bentham gives a list of excusing circumstances which is much the same as that given by most writers on the subject, but the novelty of his account lies in his undertaking to justify the list in terms of strict Utilitarianism. In cases where there is Unintentionality, Unconsciousness (i.e. ignorance of some criminative circumstance), or Mis-supposal (i.e. mistaken belief in the presence of some exculpative circumstance) he holds that punishment must be inefficacious, and that the act must therefore be excused.[1]

Now our concern is not with the propriety of legal punishment for unintentional acts, but whether they are due for moral blame. It is true that it is only in the course of discussing principles concerning punishment that Bentham states that unintentionality is an excusing condition, but it seems reasonable to think that he would look on it as morally excusing also. For one thing, he is working out his theory in the light of his single criterion, the Principle of Utility; and for him this is a moral criterion. Furthermore, in an earlier chapter, after putting forward rules for deciding the presence and degree of intentionality of an act, he declares that they are 'of the most extensive and constant application, as well to moral discourse as to legislative practice'. It seems fair to conclude, then, that Bentham is indeed concerned with the question to which we are at present addressing ourselves.

His answer to that question is not clear. At one place, we have seen, he says that an unintentional act is excused from blame. At another, however, speaking of omissions, he says that:

Even though the mind should never have had the incident in contemplation (insomuch that the event of its not happening should not have been so much as obliquely intentional),

the omission is still an act, in the sense of 'act' required for an offence, and it is strictly culpable.[2] In a third place, he seems prepared to take a position between these two extremes: in almost all cases, he says, the absence of intentionality will constitute grounds of extenuation.[3] This confusion may be

[1] p. 174.   [2] p. 72, n. 1.   [3] p. 96.

partly due to two linguistic ambiguities to which Bentham alludes once or twice in passing, but does not pause to sort out. If we do so, we shall be better placed to answer the question ourselves.

First, there is the ambiguity of the word *unintentional*. It is sometimes assumed that every act which is in any way attributed to a human agent must be either intentional or unintentional, i.e. that these two terms are contradictories. But suppose we translate 'A's act in doing X was intentional' as

(1) A intended to do X, and (2) A did X.

Then the contradictory of (1) is

(3) A did not intend to do X;

it is not

(4) A intended not to do X.

(3) can be verified if A elicited, or had, no intention whatever to do X or anything else: if he was asleep, or unconscious. (4) is verified only if A did elicit, or have, an intention: a particular intention: the intention, namely, not-to-do-X. Now, unfortunately, the word *unintentional* applies both to (3) and (4). The adjective *unintentional* is used both of an act which I did, though I did not intend to do it, and of an act which in some sense 'I did', though I intended not do to it.

There is a further reason for saying that *intentional* and *unintentional* are not contradictories; there are some acts which, in contemporary usage, are not naturally called either intentional, or unintentional. I may know that when I start my car on a cold morning it back-fires; but one would not normally say that I produced that effect intentionally: nor would it be said that I did so unintentionally.

The equation

$$\text{Intentional} : \text{Unintentional} :: p : \text{not-}p$$

is therefore false. But even if the equation were true, there is one conclusion that would not follow: viz., that since one is responsible for what one does intentionally, one is not responsible for what one does unintentionally: from 'If p, then q', one cannot conclude, 'But not-p; therefore not-q'. The confusion sometimes appears less flagrantly, in pleas such as, 'A is not to be blamed for doing X, because he did it unintentionally'. The reasoning latent in this seems to be somewhat as follows:

> If A intends not to do X, then he is not to be blamed if X happens;
> therefore, if A does X unintentionally, he is not to be blamed for it;
> therefore, if A does not intend to do X, he is not to be blamed for it.

There are two difficulties in this. First, the first step overlooks the fact that one may be blamed not only for negligence in intention and attention to one's duties, but also for negligence in the manner of the performance, or even in undertaking the act at all: the young driver who plays 'chicken' intends to go as close to the other car as possible without hitting it, but that does not excuse him if an accident takes place. Second, the protasis, 'If I intend not to do X', is not identical with the protasis, 'If I do not intend to do X'; hence, they do not license the inferring of identical apodoses. The fact that the same word *unintentional* applies to the two different protases creates the danger of our always inferring from it the same apodosis; to make identical inferences from them is to argue

If p, then q; but r; therefore q.

A second ambiguity concerns such words as *voluntary*, *involuntary*, and their adverbs. We have a number of rough and ready rules of thumb, such as, 'A person cannot be blamed for X if he did not do X voluntarily'. Now the phrase 'did not do X voluntarily' is very loose indeed. Bentham notices the ambiguity, and gives it as his reason for preferring to discuss the conditions of culpability in terms of the *intentional* rather than the *voluntary*. The latter he declares to be triply ambiguous, being synonymous sometimes with *intentional*, sometimes with *uncoerced*, and sometimes with *spontaneous*. Of the first of these he writes: 'By a voluntary act is meant sometimes any act in the performance of which the will has had any concern at all: in this sense it is synonymous to *intentional*.'[1]

This is the only place where Bentham tells us what he means by 'intentional', although it is quite in keeping with his frequent insistence that acts and consequences alone are intentional, and circumstances not: since the former two alone are objects of the will, the latter of the understanding only. We have already found that this assertion itself raises problems, since he frequently refers to intentionality as a circumstance; if one cannot intend circumstances, therefore one cannot intend intentionally. Now we must try to discover what Bentham means by 'an object of the will', or what it is for 'the will to have any concern in the performance of an act'.

Bentham appears to presuppose the theory that a voluntary act is an act which has a special sort of pre-existing cause: a volition, or act of the will: whenever I voluntarily X, I first will to X; then, as a result, I X. In one form or another the theory has had many advocates. It is exemplified in Hume's definition of the will as 'the internal impression we feel and are conscious of when we knowingly give rise to any new motion of our body or new perception of our mind'. Let us quote again from Austin's version: he, incidentally, acknowledged his having derived it from the *Inquiry into the Relation of Cause and Effect* of Thomas Brown, the Edinburgh philosopher, physiologist, and poet. Austin wrote:

Certain movements of our bodies follow invariably and *immediately* our wishes and desires for these *same* movements. . . . These antecedent wishes and these consequent movements are human *volitions* and *acts* (strictly and properly so called). . . . Our

[1] p. 82, n. 1.

desires of those bodily movements which immediately follow our desires for them are the only *volitions*; or (if you prefer the expression better) the only acts of the will. . . . A voluntary movement of my body, or a movement which follows a volition, is an *act*. . . . The act itself is *intended* as well as *willed*. . . . A consequence of the act is never willed.[1]

Mill said bluntly that a volition is 'simply a physical cause: our will causes our bodily actions in the same sense, and in no other, in which cold causes ice and a spark causes an explosion of gun-powder'.[2] Such views have given rise, of course, to many objections. I have voluntarily written every word on this page; but I have not been conscious of a corresponding number of impressions, produced a corresponding number of desires, or elicited a corresponding number of volitions: or would there be, on the theory of these philosophers, a volition per letter? A picture held them captive, the para-mechanical picture of voluntary action: the pen moves because my hand pushes it; my hand moves because my will pushes it. It is from this picture of the will as a quasi-mechanical cause of voluntary acts, 'a motor without mass and without inertia', that Wittgenstein was particularly concerned to disenthral us.

Now, as we saw in Chapter 1, Austin's account gives a theory of what things count as acts, as well as of what it is for an act to be voluntary; and on the first of these, I think, Bentham does not share his views. Where wrongful conduct at least is in question, Bentham would draw the line between 'act' and 'consequences', not at the point where muscular control ends, but at the point where harm begins; his act-terms embrace a much wider range of elements than do Austin's. Nor does he share Austin's account of the relationship between 'will' and 'intend'. For Bentham, both terms may be applied both to an act and to its consequences; for Austin, 'will' applies only to acts, 'intend' applies only to consequences. But on the point that concerns us here, they

[1] Loc. cit.   [2] *System of Logic* (ed. London, 1898), p. 232.

are at one; Bentham appears to agree that a voluntary act is one that follows and is caused by an act of the will. For there are several places in which Bentham seems to assume of all acts what he says explicitly of acts of omission: in the course of defending the linguistic oddity of speaking of the motive for an omission, which etymologically seems to involve the concept of moving one not to move, he says that even an omission, or the forbearance from action,

supposes an act done, when such forbearance is voluntary. It supposes, to wit, an act of the will, which is as much a positive act, as much a motion, as any other act of the thinking substance.[1]

Since this doctrine has been disposed of, successfully as it seems to me, by Wittgenstein, Ryle, Hart, and Miss Anscombe, there is no need to pursue it here. I shall simply say a little more about the term 'voluntary' and show why I do not think that culpability is restricted to those acts for which the agent has antecedently elicited a desire—whether a volition or an intention.

The first thing to remark is that, in the case of the word *voluntary* and its derivatives, one of the reasons for the ambiguities in the word *intentional* and its derivatives does not obtain. The words *intentional, intentionality, unintentional,* and so on, derive from the transitive verb *to intend,* and are commonly used to qualify or amplify some act or object which is, or is not, intended by some agent. In the case of the word *voluntary* and its derivatives, this is not so. Etymologically it may be traced back through the French *volontaire* to the Latin *voluntas,* to the present participial stem *volent-* of *velle,* the verb *to will.* But in English usage we have no inclination to translate phrases containing *voluntary, involuntary,* &c., into phrases containing some corresponding verb; whereas we do readily re-state phrases containing *intentional, unintentional,* &c., in synonymous phrases containing the verb to *intend.* Furthermore, even if, for some unusual purpose, we were to draw on the possible verb-candidate *to will*, its transitive use does not have the meaning required. It may be used of divine or royal desires, with the same archaic flavour of such phrases as 'it is our pleasure that . . .', or in 'God wills all men to be saved'; it may be used as humorous over-statement, as in *Lucky Jim*: 'When sherry was brought round, Dixon willed his arm to remain by his side until his seniors had taken a glass'; it may make a facetious claim to telepathic causal influence, as when an anguished golfer says that his opponent willed a putt into the hole; it may be an unidiomatic rendering of a proverb from a foreign language, as in 'He that wills the end, wills the means.' But what the word does not do is offer a transitive verb to play the role in an alternative, translated, version which the adjective *voluntary* plays in the original phrase: 'In doing X, I acted quite voluntarily' cannot be literally translated, for instance, 'I willed X'. It is true that the puzzles about the meaning of 'I did not intend to X' have no counterpart in discussions of voluntary action; but then, the latter have not the advantages sometimes gained by re-stating the phrase in verb-form.

We may see, then, that an equation such as

Involuntary : Voluntary :: Unintentional : Intentional

is false. The word *unintentional* is in some sense—or rather, as we have seen, in two senses—a negation of *intentional*; but the word *involuntary*, as actually used, tends to be a word *sui juris*: as the late Professor Austin said, 'voluntarily' and 'involuntarily', in spite of their apparent connexion, are fish from very different kettles. The characteristic application of 'involuntary' is to reflex actions, such as jerking the foot when the knee is tapped or jumping when startled by an explosion, or to things such as sneezing. If one has shot a person without meaning to do so, one would quite naturally protest that one had done it *unintentionally*, if it had happened through faulty aim when shooting at something else, or through having mistakenly believed that the gun was unloaded, or through having unexpectedly twitched or started with one's finger on the trigger; but to say that one had done it *involuntarily* would be to suggest that only some explanation such as the last was the case, i.e. that one had twitched or started with one's finger on the trigger, through reflex action or unexpected fright or the like.

Perhaps some confusion in these matters arises from the mistaken belief that whatever applies to Aristotle's ἑκούσιον and ἀκούσιον applies in the same way to the English *voluntary* and *involuntary*. To be sure, Aristotle put us on our guard with his own distinction between ἀκούσιον and οὐχ ἑκούσιον. This is not to imply that his ἀκούσιον has the narrow use which I have claimed for *involuntary*, but to notice that he has warned us that ἀκούσιον is not the simple contradictory of ἑκούσιον. Furthermore, there are many acts which Aristotle would call ἑκούσια, and which we should consider fit candidates for praise or blame, to which none the less we should not naturally apply the term 'voluntary', or 'voluntarily': nor, of course, would we call them 'involuntary'; I mean, for instance, those cases in which Aristotle speaks of a man's injuring his fellow as a culpable error when the occurrence of the harm is not contrary to reasonable expectation, but is done without evil intent. For, as a rule, we use the words 'voluntary' and 'voluntarily' only to rebut a suggestion, or dispel a misconception, that some factor or consideration required for morally responsible action was lacking. Similarly, I think, we use such phrases as 'But it was not a voluntary act' only when we wish to rebut the presumption that all such factors were present. The fact that jurists and philosophers have often been out of step with ordinary language on this point, speaking as if only voluntary acts can be blameworthy, may be due in part to the terminology of the scholastics. They held that only a *voluntarium* could be laid to the agent's moral account; but their *voluntarium* was practically identical with Aristotle's ἑκούσιον, not with the 'voluntary act' of English usage. If a signalman, through culpable inadvertence, forgets to change a signal, they would call his omission a *voluntarium*; but it would be odd for us to call it voluntary. The scholastic terminology is exemplified by Aquinas's remark that an act is called voluntary, either because it falls under an act of the will, or because it falls within the power of the will (*cadit sub potestate voluntatis*).

The most important cases which illustrate these points are those which come under the heading of Negligence. We must pay some attention to that subject a little later; but here we may anticipate one point. It is a fact that we do blame people for doing damage, not intentionally, but through negligence. It may be for an act of commission, as when a motorist carelessly drives into a car legitimately parked by a kerb; it may be for an act of omission, as with the signalman who forgets that a train is due to pass and fails to change a signal. Such acts, or omissions, will be blamed if (though only if) it was in the power of the agent to perform, or not to perform, them. We say that the agent was responsible, or was to blame, since the act, or the avoidance of damage, was in his power; but we do not say that it was 'voluntary'. A case of negligence may have been due to culpable inadvertence, and, even though it was therefore unintentional, the subject of severe moral censure; but we do not apply the word 'voluntary' to it. One could, no doubt, serve notice of calling such cases 'voluntary'; but one would then be departing from ordinary usage. It was suggested above that some acts, or consequences of acts, are properly called neither intentional nor unintentional; e.g. producing the back-fire which one knows always occurs when one starts one's car on a cold morning. Similarly, I think, such acts, or consequences of acts, are called neither voluntary nor involuntary; but one is certainly responsible for producing them, and if such production were to come under some rubric of moral censure (e.g. startling a dangerously ill person), then one could be blamed for it.

What is required for an act to be culpable, then, is not that it be voluntary, in Bentham's sense that the voluntary 'supposes an act of the will'; but simply that it lie within the agent's power to do it, or not to do it, as the relevant moral rule requires. In another place, Bentham appears to hold that this was sufficient; in arguing for the view that an inadvertent omission can be culpable, he says:

The state the person's mind was in at the time when, if he *had* so willed, the incident might have happened, is in many cases productive of as material consequences; and not only as likely, but as fit to call for the interposition of other agents, as the opposite one.[1]

Here Bentham seems to admit, as in some places he appears to deny, that an offence can be present even when there has been no act of the will, nor any other sort of mental act; what is necessary is the power, the ability, and the opportunity to act. This, then, is the conclusion to which our inquiry seems to lead: what is required for moral blame is not the intention or the will or the desire to do what is wrong, but the ability not to do it.

(ii) *Consciousness*

An important factor that may affect a person's 'ability' in the sense thus required is his unawareness of some element in the situation: 'I wot that through ignorance ye did it', is one of the classic pleas for excuse. We must now therefore take up that question, and again the discussion is fruitfully opened with Bentham's account. He devotes a chapter to the subject under the title 'Consciousness', and gives other rules and arguments in the chapters that deal with Consequences, and 'Cases Unmeet for Punishment'. His doctrine may be summarized under three headings.

[1] p. 72, n. 1.

First, terminology: Bentham speaks of an act's being unadvised or misadvised, rather than of an agent's acting in ignorance or error. He calls an act advised, unadvised, or misadvised, with regard to a given circumstance, according as the agent is aware, unaware, or mistakenly persuaded of the existence of that circumstance, or of its materiality to a given consequence. The nouns which he uses as corresponding to these adjectives are advisedness, unadvisedness, and mis-supposal. Unadvisedness concerning a criminative circumstance will be heedless, and mis-supposal concerning an exculpating (justifying) circumstance will be rash, in cases where a person of ordinary prudence and benevolence would have devoted such reflection to the circumstances as would have effectually disposed him to prevent the mischievous action from taking place.[1]

Second, Bentham gives a rule for the connexion between Consciousness and Intentionality: Provided there be no mis-supposal, advisedness with regard to the presence of a given circumstance, and its materiality to a given consequence, extend the intentionality from the act to that consequence. If Tyrrel's *act* of shooting the arrow was intentional, and advised as to the circumstances of its likely direction and speed, the King's approach, and so on, then the *consequence* of the King's death was also intentional. 'Perhaps he did not positively wish it; but for all that, in a certain sense he intended it.'[2]

Third, the connexion between Consciousness and Culpability: Bentham's rules may be given under four headings. (1) Ignorance (i.e. unadvisedness or mis-supposal) is itself culpable when attended with heedlessness or rashness.[3] (2) The presence of consciousness with regard to such or such a circumstance is an essential ingredient in the composition of this or that offence; its absence, or the presence of mis-supposal, constitutes grounds of extenuation.[4] (3) Ignorance

[1] pp. 89–92.   [2] p. 92.   [3] pp. 164–5.   [4] p. 96.

of the Law excuses the person who breaks it, if anything has been omitted which is needed to inform him of all cases which fall under it.[1] (4) Ignorance of Fact excuses where there is unconsciousness of a criminative circumstance, or mis-supposal concerning an exculpating one.[2]

Some criticisms of these rules suggest themselves. If, as Rule Two holds, the presence of consciousness of a certain circumstance is an essential ingredient of a certain offence, then its absence should exculpate; yet it is said only to extenuate. It is true that Rules Three and Four actually refer only to exemption from punishment under the law. But Rule Four is based, of course, on the Principle of Utility, which is Bentham's universal moral criterion as well as the first axiom of his legal theory; it therefore seems reasonable to put these rules forward as Bentham's conditions for moral culpability too. Hart has claimed that Bentham's argument for Rule Four, from the point of view of legal theory, rests on 'a spectacular non-sequitur', for it would show that not *punishment*, but the *threat* of punishment, must be inefficacious in such circumstances.[3] But the paragraph also contains an oddity from the point of view of our own inquiry: it holds that an act is excused if unintentional, because it is thereby unconscious; and no reason is given for excusing an unconscious act. But surely the reason one would be inclined to expect is that an unconscious act is thereby unintentional. The second of Bentham's rules quoted above is in keeping with that expectation, though it seems to be a further defect in his account that it does not strictly warrant it; it gives a rule for the intentionality of consequences when the act is advised, but none for the cases in which the act is unadvised or misadvised. 'If p, then q', Bentham tells us; but our question is, 'What if not-p?'

[1] p. 173.
[2] p. 174. To be consistent with his own terminology given earlier Bentham should have written 'unadvisedness' instead of 'unconsciousness'.
[3] 'Prolegomenon to the Principles of Punishment', *P.A.S.*, Oct. 1959, p. 18.

However, it is not our purpose to criticize Bentham's doctrine in detail, but to use it to open the question of the bearing of consciousness on the moral culpability of an act; and we may contrast Bentham with Aristotle. For Aristotle, it is particular ignorance, ἡ καθ' ἕκαστα ἄγνοια, ignorance of particular factual circumstances, which excuses an agent and renders his act blameless. Five factual considerations are mentioned as things of which the agent may be ignorant, and the act thereby excused; Aristotle here offers no rules for deciding whether such ignorance may itself be culpable, as a result of negligence; he says simply that such ignorance excuses. But general ignorance, ignorance of the universal, ἡ καθόλου ἄγνοια, far from excusing the act, is itself blame-worthy, and marks the agent as a wicked man.[1] One may feel that this is not so much a case of ignorance as of error; it is not so much that the wicked man is ignorant of the true moral principles as that he embraces false ones; as Nowell-Smith says, he 'adopts and adheres to bad moral principles'.[2] But the point is clear. Apparently Himmler believed that it was his duty to kill Jewish people; and Aristotle would say that, far from excusing his genocidal acts, his holding such a belief branded him a wicked man. Bentham, on the other hand, seems to hold that ignorance of the law always excuses,[3] and that ignorance of fact[4] excuses, except where it arises from heedlessness or rashness: for these alone are argued to be culpable, and other cases of unadvisedness or mis-supposal are held to excuse.[5] Indeed, the Latin terminology put forward by Bentham suggests that ignorance is culpable only when it arises from heedlessness, and that error is culpable only when it arises from rashness.[6] This seems very odd

---

[1] *Eth. Nic.*, 1110^b 31 f.   [2] *Ethics* (London, 1954), p. 265.

[3] That is, if the penal provision has not been made known to the agent, he is not to be punished. Bentham's opinion concerning mistakes in moral principle is not so clear.

[4] i.e. unadvisedness or mis-supposal concerning some factual circumstance.   [5] pp. 164–5, 174.   [6] p. 95, n. 3.

indeed. Were Himmler's crimes, then, simply cases of heed-lessness, or rashness?

In moral and legal theory the distinction of ignorance into Ignorance of (or Error concerning) Fact, and Ignorance of (or Error concerning) Law, is a hallowed one. But in practice, it is not in these terms that we approach a particular case. Suppose that A is admitted to have killed B by giving him dropwort, a plea for excuse on the score of ignorance might take several forms: A did not (*a*) know, or (*b*) realize, or (*c*) think, or (*d*) believe, or (*e*) remember, or (*f*) advert to the fact, that (1) killing is wrong; or (2) killing a person such as B (e.g. a tyrant) is wrong; or (3) that dropwort is a deadly poison; or (4) that the substance he gave to B was dropwort; or (5) that his act was that of giving it to B. The next step will not be to arrange the thirty possible combinations into so many cases of 'Ignorance of Fact', and so many cases of 'Ignorance of Law': and then to conclude to A's guilt or innocence according to the column in which his particular case falls. Rather, if we use the variable 'N' for the thirty different possible combinations of verb-terms and predicate-terms just listed, then the sort of conclusion towards which the inquiry must work is *either*, 'But he should have N-ed'; or, 'It was his business to N'; or, 'There is no excuse for his not N-ing': *or*, 'He could not have N-ed'; or, 'He could not be expected to N'; or, 'It was not his fault that he did not N'. In the ordinary language of day-to-day moral evaluation, we speak as if ignorance (or error, or oversight, or forgetfulness, and so on) excuses or fails to excuse, not according as it bears upon matters of moral rule, law, or principle, or upon matters of relevant fact: but according as the ignorance it-self is or is not culpable. It is true that, in order to reject an excuse put forward on grounds of ignorance, one might argue that the ignorance in question was a case of ignorance of moral principle, and invoke an ethical theory which held that such ignorance is always culpable; but the point in making such moves would be to show that the ignorance in question was itself culpable. This may arise in three types of case, which we shall take up in turn.

1. There is the case in which a person sees the need to inform himself of some factual aspect of a situation but does not do so. This occurs characteristically in that type of negligence in which the agent realizes that an act of the kind which he contemplates may have harmful consequences, but instead of investigating whether they are likely to arise on this occasion, decides to 'go ahead and take the risk'. This may arise with either deed or omission. A person may realize that doing-X is the sort of thing which may lead to harmful consequences, but not bother to inform himself of the facts on the present occasion: for instance, a motorist drives over a busy crossing without stopping to see whether the road is clear, or a game-hunter fires at a movement in the bush without knowing whether it is caused by game or by a native beater. He may realize that not-doing-X may have harmful consequences, but decide to act without making sure: for instance, a lighthouse-keeper decides to finish his game of cards, although he cannot quite remember if he is due back; or a surgeon begins an operation, although he realizes that he has not assured himself of the patient's heart-condition. If harm follows in such cases, it will arise from ignorance (for it is assumed that if the agent *knew* that damage would be done on this occasion he would not perform, or omit, the action); but the ignorance does not excuse him, for he is himself to blame for it: the ignorance itself is culpable.

2. There are cases in which a person holds sound general moral principles, and is correctly informed of all the relevant facts of the situation, but is mistaken in his application of the principles to the facts. Two people may subscribe to the same moral code, and agree on all the facts of a given case, yet disagree in their verdict upon it; they may disagree as to how a rule is to be applied, or as to which rule is the relevant one,

or as to which of two rules, admittedly correct in isolation but apparently incompatible on the present occasion, should take priority.

The problem is rather like that discussed by Prichard and Ross, 'Should one fulfil one's objective or subjective duty?'[1] It is not quite the same problem, for they were concerned with Ignorance of Fact; thus Ross says:

> The objective element consists of the facts about the various persons and things involved in the situation, in virtue of which a certain act would in fact be the best possible fulfilment of the various *prima facie* obligations resting on the agent. . . . The subjective element consists of the agent's thoughts about the situation.[2]

One puzzling element in that discussion is the implication that the agent has to make a choice: which should he do— what is objectively, or what is, subjectively, his duty? on which should he act, the facts as they really are, or the facts as he believes them to be? There is a false suggestion here. The person is not confronted with two versions of the facts between which he must choose; a person sees the facts only as *he* sees the facts, and not as someone else sees them. Nevertheless, someone else *can* see them; and an observer will often be in a position to say that the agent has acted on a false appraisal of the situation. Such an observer will not say of the mistaken man, 'He did his subjective duty'; but rather, 'He is excused for not doing his duty'. The description 'doing his subjective duty' incorporates a confusion of 'excuse' and 'justification'. The person who, after taking due care, arrives at a false appraisal of the facts is excused if he acts upon it; but his act is not *justified*. We are not saying that we regret that the situation has arisen, but given that it has, this act became the right thing to do; we are saying that the

---

[1] H. A. Prichard, 'Duty and Ignorance of Fact', in his *Moral Obligation* (Oxford, 1949), pp. 18–38; W. D. Ross, *Foundations of Ethics* (Oxford, 1939), pp. 145–56.

[2] Ross, p. 156.

act remains a wrongful act, but given the circumstances, the agent is not to be blamed for it.

Our own problem is a little different from that one, and a little more vexed. There is no reason to think that an observer is more likely to be right than the agent; both have full access to, and by hypothesis are agreed upon, general moral principles and all the facts of the case. Perhaps we could say that disagreement occurs, not at the stage of applying general moral principles to an individual case, but at the intermediate stage of formulating principles of less extensive applicability. Moralists have often argued whether the duty to keep a promise should take priority over the duty to perform an urgent act of charity, or the obligation to keep a secret over the obligation not to lie. Such arguments may end in conclusions which are less general than 'One should keep one's promises', but more general than 'Here and now, on this particular occasion, I am not bound to keep the promise I made to meet X at place p and time t.' It may be advanced, in the course of the argument, that when two morally responsible people make an appointment to meet for some form of entertainment, there is an implicit understanding that the obligation thus created does not override the general obligation to assist a person suddenly taken ill; and this sort of conclusion may be embodied in some proposition, less general than 'One should keep one's promises', or 'One should help a person in urgent need', but still a general principle; should we call it an 'applied principle'?

Conflict may also arise between moral principles even more general. Two people may subscribe to the principles 'One must not do evil that good may come' and 'One should always choose the lesser of two evils'; they may agree about all the relevant facts of a situation; but they may disagree as to which of the two principles is applicable. C. P. Snow has written about the disagreement between Sir Henry Tizard and Professor Lindemann concerning the proposal to bomb the homes of German munition-workers in the hope of crippling German military production. Apparently their disagreement was simply technical and factual; would the losses incurred in such bombing be significantly outweighed by the damage done to the German war effort? But one can imagine two people debating the morality of the proposal. 'You must not do evil that good may come', says one person; 'the end of the operation, i.e. winning the war, is a worthy one, but it is wrong to seek this end by immoral means, viz. the bombing of non-combatants, including many women and children.' 'I agree that one must not do evil that good may come', rejoins the other; 'but that principle is not at issue in this proposal. In modern war munition-workers are in no different case from combatants in uniform, and the death of women or children present in the bombed areas is not a means to our end; our end would be achieved just as well if they had all been evacuated. The point is, one should choose the lesser of two evils; in the long run, more lives will be saved, and victory will come more surely and more soon, if we bomb the German workers' homes.' Such an argument need not be restricted to an individual case; it may be in such terms as, 'The morality of saturation-bombing': not as general as, 'One must not do evil that good may come', or even, 'One is not entitled to kill enemy non-combatants', but sufficiently general to be called an argument over moral principle.

Ethical Cognitivists, or at any rate Objectivists, would hold that their answers to such questions are either correct or mistaken. One may not feel oneself able to pontificate about which answer is the correct one; nevertheless, some of the views held are mistaken, and some—or at least one—correct. What then are we to make of Aristotle's contention that ignorance—and therefore, presumably, error—concerning a moral principle, far from excusing a man, is itself blame-worthy and constitutes vice? At what level of logical generality is that true? If the man believes that one should commit murder when one can get away with it, Aristotle's principle is clearly applicable; but what if he believes that saturation-bombing, or therapeutic abortion, or tyrannicide, is not murder? In these cases we are troubled by one aspect of the problem that Prichard and Ross considered: there is no reason why the onlooker should be more confident of correct judgement than the agent himself, when the morality of such questions is disputed within their own community. A man is wicked, says Nowell-Smith, if he adopts and adheres to bad moral principles; but this does not mean that I brand as wicked colleagues and neighbours who do not share my views on moral issues seriously disputed and debated in our community. But we can also think of cases when all, or practically all, the members of our own community are agreed that a policy, i.e. a rather specific principle, espoused in another country is morally unsound. The South African Government's policy of *apartheid* is a case in point. Dr. Verwoerd agrees that all men must be accorded their rights, and that injustice is always wrong; but he denies that *apartheid* is unjust. This is the sort of case we are considering; we may assert quite confidently that a person's opinion is morally wrong, though not denying that he is quite sincere in upholding it; can we exempt him from blame on the score of ignorance or error?

To answer this, one need not claim to be able to draw up one list of moral principles of which inculpable ignorance is possible, and another of which it is not. The conditions necessary for holding ignorance or error to be culpable can be stated only in general terms: A's ignorance or error about X is culpable if and only if X is something which A is (1) obliged, and (2) able, to know. Now by hypothesis the disputed point is something which he is obliged to know; we are obliged to know what is morally required of us. But if a person has addressed himself to a disputed moral issue, considered the arguments of those opposed to his view and answered them to his own satisfaction, perhaps even suffered material loss for holding to his point of view, then the matter is something which he (*he*: given his intelligence, moral maturity, upbringing, and environment) is not able to learn. As Reid says:

When a man must act . . . he ought surely to use all the means in his power to be rightly informed. When he has done so, he may still be in an error; but it is an invincible error, and cannot justly be imputed to him as a fault.[1]

Of course, if a person refuses to consider the arguments brought against his position for fear that they might shake a treasured prepossession, or if he considers them with a closed mind, or without due care and attention, then the ignorance or error itself is culpable, and cannot excuse the act which arises from it. At the same time, it is not suggested that the person should act against his mistaken though sincere convictions: conscientiousness, in the sense of 'following the dictates of conscience', or acting in accordance with what one believes to be one's duty, is a necessary condition of any proper conduct; what such a person should do is, not act against his mistaken beliefs, but correct them. But if he has examined his convictions with all the care that the situation warrants, and to the best of his ability, then, as Reid says, 'I see not wherein he is to be blamed.' To say this is not to say that the act done in inculpable ignorance ceases to be wrongful, but simply that the agent is not to be blamed for it: it is an excusing, rather than a justifying, circumstance. One may express a qualified esteem for some other aspect of the agent's behaviour: one may say, for instance, 'I cannot condone A's action, but I do admire the courage with which he stood by his principles'; but one does not alter one's conviction that

[1] *Essays on the Active Powers*, v, in the *Works* (Edinburgh, 1863), vol. ii, p. 647.

the act which he performed was wrong. Where ignorance is culpable, says Aristotle, the agent acts ἀκουσίως; whereas only ἑκούσια are good (or bad). I should think that this principle is quite rightly applied to any case where ignorance or error is in fact blameless.

3. The other difficult case is that of Inadvertence. There is sometimes a reluctance to admit, in the abstract, that a person may be blamed for inadvertent acts, whether of commission or omission; perhaps this is partly due to a reluctance to think that one can incur moral guilt without being aware of it. Nevertheless we frequently *do* blame people for acts done, or omitted, through inadvertence. We do not simply exonerate the motorist who does not even think of the danger of driving into a busy road without slackening speed, or of driving when liable to sudden illness, or the doctor and lighthouse-keeper who simply do not think of the possible consequences of their absence from duty. To the plea 'I'm so sorry, I just did not think', the answer will often be, not 'Oh I see; then you are not to blame', but 'That's no excuse; you *should* have thought; a person in such a position has a *duty* to think'.

Now first, what are the things to which one may fail to advert? (1) One may fail to advert to the existence of an obligation. By this is meant, not that one sometimes forgets that certain kinds of action are wrong, or obligatory, but that one sometimes forgets that some particular action is required of one here and now. In the field of civil law, one does not forget that one must stop at a red traffic light; but one may fail to notice that there are now traffic lights at a familiar crossing where previously there were none. Similarly, in the field of morality, one does not forget that one must keep one's promises, but may forget that some particular promise which one has made is here and now due for fulfilment. (2) One may fail to advert to 'the nature and quality of the act', as distinct from its immoral character: i.e. I may fail to notice what it is that I am doing, so that the act is inadvertent under some relevant description. A person idly plays with a lever; he does not advert to the fact that he is pulling the trigger-release for a paper-guillotine, or of a dynamiting-device in a quarry. (3) One may fail to notice some fact which renders the act inadvertent under some important moral specification; and this is quite a common type of case. Aeschylus knew what he was saying about the Mysteries of Demeter, but did not advert to its being secret; a confidential secretary may knowingly give information, but forget that it has recently been put on the 'classified' list. A doctor gives a blood transfusion, not adverting to the fact that the patient is of an Rh blood-group. A person makes a disparaging remark about a racial or religious or political group, not adverting to the fact that his companion belongs to the group: the apology, 'I'm so sorry; I had no intention of offending you; I just did not remember that you are an X', will not set matters right; it may well aggravate them. Here again the point is not that the agent forgets the relevant moral principle or rule, viz. that it is wrong to break secrets, or endanger life, or offend one's companions; the point is that the agent fails to advert to some element of his act which causes it to fall into a category of acts thus forbidden. (4) One may fail to advert to the likely consequences of one's act. I did not realize, until it was too late, that my saying X would enable people to deduce Y, which was a secret; I fired a gun at a tree in the front garden, not stopping to think that I might miss and the bullet fly out into a busy street; I go ahead with a financial merger, not bothering my head that it may involve many people in unemployment and hardship; I freely and unreservedly air my opinions and dissatisfactions on all occasions, not considering that it is leading to unhappiness and killing affection in the home. It is not always easy to distinguish between cases of (2) and (4); if I reverse out of the garage without noticing that one of the children is playing immediately behind a back wheel, do I fail to advert to my *act*, viz. running over the child; or is this a *consequence* of the act, viz. backing the car? For Bentham, of course, the former; an act begins to have consequences at the point where it begins to do harm. My own discussions in Chapter 1 would suggest that one may quite properly say either. But disagreements on that point need not delay us here, for the conditions in which inadvertence is culpable will be practically the same in each of the four types of case we have noticed. For at the relevant moment Inadvertence and Ignorance stand alike with regard to the circumstance which Bentham calls Consciousness; and hence A's not adverting to X will be culpable if and only if X is something to which A is (1) obliged, and (2) able, to advert: whichever of the four X may be.

The first of the four—that namely in which one fails to remember that a certain act is here and now required of one— calls for a little further consideration, for it is under this heading that one may be tempted to harbour sceptical doubts about liability for culpable inadvertence. It was contended a little earlier that if a person is to be held responsible, and blamed, for some act or omission or consequence, it is not necessary that he should have desired, intended, or 'willed' the ensuing harm, but simply that it was in his power to prevent it. But surely it is 'in our power' to deal only with possibilities of acting which occur to us. In what sense was it 'in our power' to think about possibilities which we did not think about? Is not our suggestion a little of a piece with Bertie Wooster's 'I mused awhile; I was trying to remember something, but could not think what'? Perhaps the best account of 'He was perfectly well able to do X', or 'It was quite within his power to do X', as required for responsibility, is 'He could have done X if he had chosen'; but how could he choose, except between contemplated alternatives? as is not the case when 'the mind never had the act in question in contemplation', as Bentham says: i.e. in the case of Inadvertent Omission.

The question of Inadvertent Omission raises another point. It presents difficulties, to my mind unanswerable, for any theory which seeks an act of the will, or any other sort of mental act, as a necessary condition for culpability; and it does not sit comfortably with Bentham's principle, 'An act of some sort or other is necessarily included in the notion of every offence.' It presents, of course, even more serious difficulties for a theory, such as Austin's, which holds that a condition of an act X's being blameworthy is that the agent desired X. We blame a person for an inadvertent omission, not because of a wrongful desire, but because he failed to do what he was both able and obliged to do. For these two conditions are always necessary if a person is to be blamed for omitting to do X: (1) that he could have done X: for without that condition there can be no blame, for either deed or omission; (2) that X was something he was required to do: for without that, there is no omission. The fact that his not having done X led to harm of some sort is not of itself sufficient to constitute an immoral omission; it is necessary (we found) that X be required of this person on this occasion. To the charge, 'You did not do X', then, it is always a good defence to say, 'I did not have to', or 'I was not able'. The question now arises whether it is also a good defence to say, 'Oh dear, I am sorry; still, I cannot be blamed; the omission was quite inadvertent.'

The *stylus curiae* of our day-to-day moral appraisals insists that it is not a good defence. It simply is the case that we do blame people for omissions which are the result of inadvertence. It was found above that Bentham was in some confusion as to the general principles from which this answer is to be derived, but when he considered the question *ex professo* his answer was in line with common moral experience and practice. He writes:

Even though the mind should never have had the incident in question in contemplation the person is guilty for failing to act, for the same consequences follow as if the omission were intentional.[1]

Indeed it would seem that Bentham would think the person *equally* guilty, for he uses such phrases as 'in many cases productive of as material consequences', 'as likely', 'as fit to call for the interposition of other agents'. Now I think that it is an exaggeration to say that an unintentional omission is always *equally* as culpable as an intentional one. It is slightly mollifying to say, 'I completely forgot our appointment; I'm terribly sorry you were inconvenienced, I would not have had it happen for the world'; whereas it would be an insufferable aggravation to say, 'When it came to the point, I could not be bothered to keep our appointment, I just did not feel like coming'. But surely Bentham is right in saying that (at least some) inadvertent omissions are blameworthy: if I simply forget an appointment I have made, or a duty which I have, that of itself does not excuse me. My apology for not having X-ed, when I should have, is quite different according as X was or was not in my power at the time: but not according as the duty to X crossed my mind or not. The apology 'I'm terribly sorry: the train was delayed by floods; or, my car broke down' is normally a satisfactory excuse; whereas the statement 'I completely forget our appointment' is not. To plead that one's failure to fulfil an obligation was due to forgetfulness or oversight or some other form of inadvertence is not *eo ipso* to excuse oneself. If the inadvertence was due to one's being drunk at the relevant time, the defence will probably fail; if it was due to one's having been taken suddenly ill, it may well succeed. The question is, Was one to blame for the inadvertence? And the answer is, Yes: unless something beyond my control, and inculpably beyond my control, made it impossible for me to think of my obligation.

[1] p. 72, n. 1.

(iii) *Negligence*

Many cases of wrongful and culpable deed or omission which arise from defect of Intentionality or Consciousness are said to be 'due to negligence'. Negligence is an important concept, and many attempts to discover some special mental or interior act fail through their inability to account for it. This is true alike of, as Bentham would say, acts of the will, e.g. volitions, intentions, and desires, and acts of the understanding. Indeed, what makes Negligence particularly interesting to us here is the fact that frequently a person who is negligent does harm not through ill will, and intentionally, or consciously, but through lack of care or thought, unconsciously or unintentionally, in the sense that the harmful act or consequence is not something which the agent took himself to be doing or set out to produce. For the negligence involved in culpably inadvertent acts, whether of commission or omission, is only one kind of negligence: the failure to recall knowledge already acquired or judgements already made about some situation. A person may also be negligent in failing to acquire such knowledge or to make such judgements as the situation requires: he adverts to the possibility of harm if he acts without making certain investigations, but decides to 'go ahead and take the risk'. Again, one may be negligent in the way one acts, failing to take the precautions and exercise the care which a certain action demands. All negligence, then, involves some failure to take due care; but sometimes this consists in a person's not taking care in the way he acts, sometimes in the way he thinks, and sometimes in not having thought at all.

Bentham's account of heedlessness and rashness seems to embrace each of these kinds of negligence. He applies the term 'heedless' only to an unadvised act, i.e. an act in which the agent is unaware of the presence of some criminative circumstance; and the term 'rash' only to a misadvised act, i.e. an act in which the agent mistakenly believes in the presence of some exculpative (justifying) circumstance. Now what heedlessness and rashness have in common, says Bentham, is this: that they are present in cases where a person of ordinary benevolence and prudence would have devoted such reflection to the circumstances 'as would have effectually disposed him to prevent the mischievous action from taking place'. This seems to state the case of *Negligence* quite satisfactorily, for it seems successfully to avoid two possible mistakes: the one, suggesting that the term 'negligent' applies solely to how you think; the other, suggesting that it applies solely to how you act. Questions about negligence cannot be settled without taking both possibilities into account. A man acts negligently if, knowing that a revolver is loaded, he tosses it into the air in the presence of several people; but he also acts negligently if he does so, *not* knowing whether it is loaded. Negligence does not necessarily terminate at the point of information, or advertence, but may also terminate at the point of action; it would be negligent (short of malicious intent) to inform oneself or remind oneself carefully of the facts, and then act without regard to them.

Now even in that particular kind of negligence which consists in inadvertence, 'negligence' and 'inadvertence' are not synonymous terms, and it is useful to remark on the difference between them. To say, 'It was through inadvertence that A did X', may possibly be to exonerate him; to say that it was through negligence is certainly not. Often the plea of negligence will mitigate blame: other things being equal, to do harm through negligence is less wicked than to do harm through malice; but it *is* culpable. 'Culpable negligence' is a pleonasm: there is no such thing as inculpable negligence; but there can be inculpable inadvertence. For to say that a person acted inadvertently is simply to state a fact; to say that he acted negligently is to make, or imply, an evaluation of the facts. To say that a person acted (whether in an act of commission or omission) inadvertently is to say that he did not think of what he was doing, or of some important aspect or likely consequence of what he was doing. To substitute 'negligently' for 'inadvertently' is, again, to say that he did not think of the act or the circumstance or the consequence in question; but in addition, to say that he was both obliged and able to think of it. When we attribute negligence to a person, we are saying that he has failed to comply with a standard of conduct with which a person in his situation is both obliged and able to comply; when we attribute negligent inadvertence to a person, we are saying that he has failed to comply with a standard of thoughtfulness and attentiveness with which a person in his situation is both obliged and able to comply.

Every case of Negligence, therefore, has the features of culpable omission: it is a failure to do something which one is both obliged and able to do. Yet we have seen that Negligence may be present in acts of commission as well as in acts of omission. The resolution of this apparent paradox draws attention to two final points.

First, Negligence is not a separate moral-species, as are Murder, Theft, and Adultery; rather, it applies to certain types of failure to meet obligations connected with many different species. In the case of acts of commission, the term 'Negligence' frequently has adverbial rather than substantival implications; it does not tell us what the person's act was, but how he performed it, viz. without due care. The substantive which characterizes his offence, and tells us of what sort of wrongdoing he was guilty, will often be a species-term: e.g. manslaughter, when he drove a motor-car, or dispensed dangerous drugs, with gross negligence; breach of confidence, when he spoke of confidential matters without due care. One may say that these offences were *due to negligence* on the part of the agent: but not that the specific offence of which he was guilty was 'Negligence'. Similarly, in the case of inadvertent omissions, the rule violated is not the rule 'Since one is obliged to do X, one is obliged to advert to that obligation at the relevant time'; but simply the rule enjoining one to do X. Hence, we characterize the fault involved, not as 'Negligent Inadvertence', but as 'not having done X': e.g. not having changed a railway signal, or not having kept an appointment, or not having paid a debt. There appears to be a difference, therefore, in the language appropriate to the consequences of negligence in cases of acts of commission and acts of omission. In the former, the act is not enjoined on the agent: something concerning its consequences is. In the latter, the *act* is enjoined on him, and his negligent inadvertence leads to his not performing it; but it seems inappropriate to speak of his non-performance as a *consequence* of his inadvertence. It is the non-performance which is the offence, and it is the harm that results from that that is best spoken of as the consequence of his fault.

Second, we found in Chapter 1 that not every case in which not-doing-X had harmful consequences was a culpable omission, but only those in which doing-X was required by some moral rule. Where Negligence is present, the rule violated is that which requires a person to give thought and attention to the nature, circumstances, and likely consequences of his act, and to exercise care in performing it. But this is a peculiar sort of rule. It is not antecedent to or separate from the rule enjoining or forbidding the act in question. Just as Negligence is not a species of wrongdoing separate from Murder, Theft, and Adultery, so the rule which requires us to take due thought, and act with due care, is not a separate rule from those which command us to pay our debts and forbid us to lie. For instance, what is *not* the case is that, as well as having obligations to pay my taxes, to check my brakes, to stop at dangerous crossings, and to handle loaded guns carefully, I also have a separate, antecedent, obligation to advert to my obligation to do these things, and an obligation to take precautions against forgetting these obligations. This would open an infinite regress: I have a duty to do X; hence, I have a duty to advert to my duty to do X; hence. . . . Rather, the duty to do X includes, as part of it, the obligation to take reasonable steps against omitting X through forgetfulness or inadvertence; it does not create a separate, antecedent, obligation-to-take-precautions. One has particular obligations to do X, and Y, and Z, and a general obligation not to harm others with one's actions; and all these obligations involve attending to, thinking about, informing oneself of, and remembering, various things.

We can now see the points of resemblance and difference between Negligence-statements and Culpable-Ignorance-statements. Negligence and Culpable Ignorance are not interchangeable terms. On the one hand, there are certain types of negligence which do not involve culpable ignorance, as when one has taken due care to inform oneself of everything relevant to right action, but acted without due care. On the other hand, there are certain types of culpable ignorance which do not involve negligence: Aristotle calls the man who holds wrong moral principles μοχθηρός: Nowell-Smith calls him 'wicked', and, though he expresses dissatisfaction about this word where minor defects are in question, no one would suggest 'negligent' as the *mot juste*: Himmler's crimes did not arise from negligence. But the concept of Culpable Ignorance is similar to that of Negligence on three scores. First, it has the features of all culpable omissions, viz. it is (1) a failure to do something which is (2) possible for one to do, and (3) required of one by a moral rule. The rule has been well stated by Reid:

> Morality requires, not only that a man should act according to his judgment, but that he should use the best means in his power that his judgment be according to truth.[1]

Second, this rule is not separate from or antecedent to the rule which enjoins or forbids the act in question. It is not

[1] Loc. cit.

that, in addition to the rule forbidding the action X, there is another rule enjoining me to inform myself of the obligations not to do X, and another requiring me to remind myself of that obligation at the appropriate time, and so on: for each of these would open a regress. Rather, the rule which forbids me to do X at the same time demands my attending to, thinking about, informing myself of, various facts and rules and principles. Hence, although it is my *ignorance* which is culpable, I am blamed for the *act* which arises from it. The necessary reflection, attention, and so on, are enjoined *by the very same moral rule* which enjoins or forbids the act; the rule to reflect, inform myself, and so on, is part of the rule, 'Do X', 'Do not do Y'; hence the agent who fails to reflect, inform himself, and so on, is blamed for doing-Y, or not-doing-X. For the same reason, when ignorance is *in*culpable the agent is excused, not only for the ignorance, but also for the act to which it gives rise; it is the same rule which prescribes or forbids the act, and enjoins thought, reflection, and so on; hence, a breach which is blameless on the one score is blameless on the other. Third, it follows that Culpable Ignorance is not a separate species of wrongdoing, but applies to acts falling under many species. If through thoughtlessness I reveal information confided to me under promise of secrecy, my offence is not Culpable Thoughtlessness, but Breach of Confidence. We may say that a man's fault is *due to* culpable ignorance of one kind or another, but we say that it *is* Breach of Promise, or Damaging Another's Property, or Manslaughter.

§ 2. BEARING ON GOOD ACTS

It seems then that a person may be blamed for a wrongful act even though it was done unintentionally or unknowingly; is the same thing true when there is question of praising him for an objectively good act? Bentham has nothing to say on the question, but I think that the principal points can be made quite briefly. In short, I suggest that good and bad acts are asymmetrical with regard to the circumstances of Intentionality and Consciousness: that their absence is not always an Excusing Circumstance, but is always a Disentitling one. If an act is of a moral-species whose instances we normally call good, or if it is productive of happy consequences, three conditions seem to be necessary if it is to be held to the agent's credit: and they appear to hold for acts of performance and forbearance alike.

First, we praise a person for performing, or not performing, an act only when the performance or non-performance is intentional; we do not praise an act, however good its nature, if it is done by accident, or by mistake, or through inadvertence, or (especially in the case of omissions) through circumstances beyond the agent's control. If someone subsequently praises him for it, he will protest (rightly), 'It is no credit to me.' This will be the case, for instance, if a chemist makes a mistake in dispensing a prescription, and by some happy chance it turns out to be what the patient really needs; or if a doctor is delayed on a distant call to amputate a limb, and in the interval the damage is healed and the limb saved.

Second, acts which produce happy consequences are praiseworthy only if such consequences were in some way foreseen. For instance, I promise to send an orphan for a holiday flight in a new jet plane; in the event I do not do so, the plane crashes, and he is not aboard. This may be to my credit if my reason for changing my mind was my having conceived some doubt about the safety of the new planes, but not if the reason was belated parsimony, or my having had a quarrel with the director of the orphanage. It is not necessary that the agent foresee in detail the precise consequences that emerge, but simply that he had some idea that a certain kind of good result might be anticipated. When parents make considerable sacrifices in order to give a good education to their son, we do not deny all credit to them because they did not know that he would thus become a devoted surgeon; it was enough that they hoped to equip him to be a happy and useful member of the community.

Third, such acts are held to the agent's credit only when the happy consequences are intended (the first condition was that the *act* be intentional): and indeed, this appears to be the reason for the second condition: foresight is required, because without it the consequence would not be intentional. We have noticed that Bentham gave the opposite reason for holding a related point: an act may be excused when it is unintentional, he said, because it is thereby done in ignorance. Here, as there, I should want to disagree with him: a man is not praised for producing some consequence which he did not foresee, and the reason is rather that it is thereby unintentional. Here, indeed, the point may be made even more strongly against Bentham: it is possible for a consequence to be foreseen, yet unintended; and in that case there is no credit to the agent. This can be seen most clearly in the case of an omission, when my not doing X has two collateral consequences, Y which is harmful and Z which is good. Suppose that it is the prospect of producing Y which prompts my omission, and I foresee Z as an incidental, unintended side-effect or by-product; I may even regret Z, prefer that it not happen, assure myself that, but for the prospect of Y's being prevented, I should do X and prevent Z. In that case there is nothing laudable in my omission of X.

This third condition requires, furthermore, not only that the good consequence be intended, but also that it be intended *for its own sake*. Suppose that A, who in his undergraduate days had belonged to some Fascist or Communist organization, which he has long since quit, is about to be appointed to high office; B happens to know of A's past association, but refrains from making it known, with the result that A is appointed. This may be to B's credit; but not if his reason was the prospect of blackmailing A once he was in office.

But suppose that doing X—in the case just quoted, reporting on such past affiliations of candidates for office—were something to which B was in duty bound; then it would be much harder to admire, or even justify, his not doing X. It will often be easier for the omission of X to be justified if the obligation to do X arises from its likely benefit to A, and B feels that owing to special circumstances, not doing X would serve A even better than doing it. This will obviously be so if A approves of such a proposal, and also on many occasions even when A cannot be consulted; but the rule of thumb that suggests itself here is that it must be reasonably certain that A would agree to the suggestion if it were possible to consult him, rather than that B thinks it would be better for him that X not be done. One does not commend the paternalist employer who pays his employees less than a just wage, and spends the money thus saved on schemes of cultural uplift which *he* thinks will be better for them. In other words, it is not suggested that the three conditions held here to be necessary for an act's being adjudged good are also sufficient. To pursue this far would take us into other disputes. At one extreme, Kant thought the obligation of truth-telling so stringent that one was bound to tell a caller bent on murder that his intended victim was indeed at home, despite the fact that not telling him had the consequence of saving a life. Kant considered that such an omission would be culpable. At the opposite extreme, we have mentioned a suggestion that, given that a sheriff could save four negro lives only by 'framing' one innocent negro, failure to take this measure could be nothing less than wicked. Further, a happy consequence will much more rarely be held to the credit of the agent if it is achieved, not by his omitting an action which he is in duty bound to do, but by performing one which is forbidden. However, such problems will be better pursued in Part II; the conclusion suggested here is that a necessary condition of an agent's being praised for a good act, or consequence, is that it should have been intended by him.

This condition should not be overstated, as it is occasionally by scrupulous persons who are inclined to feel that they should be constantly making speeches to themselves about their intentions. As Hampshire has said, intentional action does not necessarily involve concurrent description or antecedent decision. It is not necessary that one give explicit formulation to one's intention; it is sufficient that it be implicit in one's conduct or part of one's plan of action. The volunteer hospital visitor does not have to elicit a new decision, or formulate some statement of intention, before beginning to speak to each patient, on pain of his act's ceasing to be commendable; the necessary intention is implicit in what he does; the act of kindness is part of his conscious plan of action. If he were asked, 'When did you form the intention of visiting that particular patient?' he would probably reject the question; but if he were asked, 'Did you mean to visit that patient?' he would answer, 'Of course.' As Wittgenstein says:

Is it correct for someone to say, 'When I gave you this rule I meant you to . . . in this case'? Even if he did not think of this case at all as he gave the rule? Of course it is correct. For 'to mean it' does not mean: 'to think of it . . .'. 'When I teach someone the formation of the series. . . . I surely mean him to write . . . at the hundredth place.'—Quite right; you meant it. And evidently without necessarily even thinking of it. This shows you how different the grammar of the verb 'to mean' is from that of 'to think of'.[1]

Now the verb *to mean* is ambiguous: sometimes it refers to the sense in which one wishes one's words to be understood, as in 'He meant "bank" in the sense of riverside'; sometimes it refers to the result one hopes to produce by one's actions, as in 'He meant to shoot the criminal, not the policeman', or in the forlorn epitaph, 'He meant well'. The verb *to intend* is similarly ambiguous: one can say, 'What exactly did you

[1] *Philosophical Investigations*, from §§ 692 and 693. I have ventured to add the inverted commas to 'think of it', and the word 'of' at the end of the quotation.

intend by that word?'; and also, 'He intended to shoot the criminal, not the policeman'. The context of this quotation suggests that Wittgenstein is referring to *meaning* in the sense of the way that one wishes one's words to be understood; but I think it quite helpful to our own discussion of *intention*, in the sense of the result one hopes to produce by one's actions; indeed, if we take *meaning* in the first sense and *intention* in the second (which is the sense relevant to our discussion), we can use the equation,

Intention : Action :: Meaning : Saying something.

Wittgenstein's passage then helps us make the point that explicitly-thinking-of-X is not a necessary condition of intending-X; and formulating a statement of intention is not necessary for an action to be intentional in the sense required for it to be adjudged morally good and held to the agent's credit.

The same passage helps us draw attention to the asymmetry of good and bad actions with regard to intentionality. If you asked the man in Wittgenstein's example, 'Did you mean me to put $(99+1)^2$ in the ninety-ninth case?' he would answer, 'Yes, of course I did.' If you asked the hospital visitor, 'Did you intend to visit that sick person you just spoke to?' he would answer, 'Yes, of course I did'; and that would be quite sufficient, without antecedent decision or explicit formulation. On the other hand, if you asked the negligent driver, 'Did you intend to knock down that pedestrian?' he would answer, 'Certainly not'; but we hold him responsible for the harm done, even so.

To sum up then, the presence of Intentionality and Consciousness is not a necessary condition for an agent's being blamed for a bad act; but it is a necessary condition for his being credited with a good one. Aquinas divided sins into three kinds: sins of ignorance, sins of weakness, and sins of malice, or ill will. In those terms we may say that there can be bad conduct without ill will; but there cannot be good conduct without good will or intention.

PART II

MOTIVES

4

MOTIVES

THE idea that a man's motive is a relevant feature in the moral evaluation of his performance is at least as old as Thrasymachus. Aristotle remarked that an adulterer will be called profligate or unjust according as he is moved by the desire for sexual pleasure or monetary gain. In the Gospels Christ frequently warned his followers that the merit of a good deed may easily be dissipated if it is done simply 'in order to be seen by men'. An extreme form of the point is found in Hume's contention that an *action* can never be the object of moral approval or disapproval; only the agent's motive, or at any rate his character, can be the object of moral appraisal. Bentham says that every kind of act is apt to assume a different character, produce different consequences, and hence have a different moral value, according to the nature of the motive which gives birth to it. Motive is the fifth of the 'articles' which he holds must always be examined in any 'transaction' on which moral judgement is to be passed.

Bentham sometimes calls Motive a Circumstance, and at that rate we should have considered it in Part I. But in Chapter I we found that it is often possible to distinguish between what-I-did and why-I-did-it. Two people may perform the same act, in the same circumstances, but with quite different motives. We shall treat Motives separately therefore in this Part II, which consists of a single chapter; and we shall discuss, first, the language of motives; second, the logic of motive-statements; and third, the effect of motive on the morality of the act which it prompts.

§ 1. THE LANGUAGE OF MOTIVES

We must begin by inquiring when it is appropriate to ask, 'What was A's motive for (in) doing X?', or to ascribe a motive to him: that is, our first question is, What sort of acts are candidates for inquiries concerning, or for the ascription of, motives?

(i) *When appropriate?*

Nowell-Smith claims that, since only what a man 'decides' or 'chooses' to do counts as an action at all, a motiveless action is logically impossible; that habit-explanations exclude choices and are therefore incompatible with the imputing of motive.[1] Thus, one does not inquire about the motives that prompt a person's habitual mannerisms: what a batsman's motive is for tapping the crease with his bat while facing up, or Churchill's for pronouncing his *r*'s as *w*'s. This stipulation successfully excludes a number of things which Bentham's preliminary, excessively loose, definition would let in:

By a motive, in the most extensive sense in which the word is ever used of a thinking being, is meant any thing that can contribute to give birth to, or even to prevent, any kind of action.[2]

At that rate, panic would be a motorist's motive for driving away without stopping after knocking down a pedestrian, drunkenness would be a man's motive for falling off his bicycle; an explosion his motive for starting out of his chair; a touch of spring weather for his behaving cheerfully at breakfast; forgetfulness for his not having kept an appointment.

---

[1] *Ethics*, pp. 124–5.   [2] p. 97.

Such things are not motives, and Nowell-Smith's proviso rightly excludes them.

But his proviso also excludes a number of things that should be included. There are many actions which do quite properly 'count as actions', but are not the outcome of decision or choice. We need not repeat the discussions of Chapter 1 on the difference between 'act' and 'action'; it is enough to recall that the only actions which count as actions in the sense relevant to morals are those which may be coupled with the possessive case of a personal noun, or a possessive pronominal adjective: 'Fenton's action', and 'my action', are actions or acts in the relevant sense; 'the action of Fenton's heart', and 'the action of my liver', are not. Now for one thing, we have found that many acts done through negligence are done without the person's deciding to do them; but they are his acts, and he is held responsible and blamed for them. It is true that they are not done for a motive, and for this fact Nowell-Smith's proviso would successfully provide; but it would also involve the false implication that they do not 'count as actions'. Besides, actions which are susceptible of habit-explanations *are* often also susceptible of motive-explanations: many an action is the outcome of a habit deliberately formed or a skill laboriously acquired, enabling one to perform a certain type of action with accuracy and success, yet without advertence or deliberate choice; nevertheless on a given occasion it is an action, and an intentional action at that. The good tennis player moves across the net to maintain approximately the same distance between himself and his partner; a trained typist turns up the paper at the end of a line; one follows the sense of a book in a foreign language—all without 'deciding' to do so. Indeed, it is often a measure of the success with which a skill has been acquired that one can, with unimpaired performance, carry out the action without grimly dredging up the appropriate resolution or making a conscious choice at all: not only in things of some muscular complexity—who ever 'decides' to throw his clutch before changing gears?—but also in things calling for self-control and virtue, such as caring for children. Yet these habitual actions count as actions; they can count as 'my actions'; if they are of moral significance, they may be held to the agent's credit or discredit; and the motive for them is often not far to seek. As Mill remarks, the will, like all other parts of our constitution, is amenable to habit. Furthermore, there are many actions done 'on impulse', and we even speak of some people as having 'impulsive' natures. This means that they often act without deliberation, but it does not mean that their actions do not count as actions; nor does it mean that they have no motive in performing them. A visitor to an orphanage may make a donation on a generous impulse, a man enlist for military service on a patriotic one; another person may do these things only after careful consideration in a cool hour; but in either case the action is 'his action', and he will often have been prompted by some motive.

Not only do such things 'count as actions', but furthermore, if interrogated, the agent could often give his reason for doing them. It would be foolish to ask, 'At what moment did you reach your decision?' to move across the net—to turn up the page—to depress the clutch-pedal before changing gear. No event of deciding occurred. But it would be perfectly in order to ask, 'Why did you do it?' The performer could quite ✳ readily, in retrospect, give his reason for each such action, though he had not explicitly formulated it for himself before the performance. When a parent is called out of bed to a child, or a priest to an accident, or a doctor to a patient, one knows quite well *why* they go; but one does not wonder at what moment they put to themselves the reason for answering the call, nor again at what moment they *decided* to go. In many, though not all, such cases the reason would be of that type of reasons we call purposes; and, indeed, it is true that only purposive action is susceptible of motive-investigation; but again, it is not necessary that the agent explicitly formulate his purpose, even 'in his own mind'. A dangerous rescue from drowning is not thought of as motiveless if the life-saver did not say to himself before diving into the water, 'I intend to save that person who is in difficulties'; nor is a bowler credited with a fluke because he did not think to himself, 'I must get this man out', but simply, 'This fellow's weak outside the off-stump.' To sum up then, we shall find that not every reason-for-acting, nor even every purpose-in-acting, is a motive; but for an investigation of motives to be appropriate at all the agent must have acted (a) intentionally, though this does not mean after a previous act of 'choosing or deciding'; and (b) for a reason or with a purpose, though this need not have been explicitly formulated, even to himself, before action.

In what sense must an action be an *action* if we are to seek its motive? How active must it be? Austin's point, that a word hardly ever shakes off its etymology, may explain our reluctance to speak of sloth as a person's motive for lying in bed: no motive without motion, we are inclined to think; and yet, we are quite clear about the motives of the inactivity of Quintus Fabius Maximus Cunctator. I think that Bentham is helpful here. He anticipates criticism for saying that a motive may determine a person 'voluntarily to forbear to act', and he replies:

Even forbearance to act, or the negation of motion (that is, of bodily motion) supposes an act done, when such forbearance is voluntary. It supposes, to wit, an act of the will, which is as much a positive act, as much a motion, as any other act of the thinking substance.[1]

I do not relish this doctrine on two scores: first, on the score of the para-mechanical picture of voluntary action as

[1] p. 98, n. 1.

triggered always by a pure volition; second, as implying that only deliberate omissions are voluntary, and hence that omissions arising out of negligence are inculpable. But I think that there is one sound point to be taken from this remark: namely, that we ascribe motives only to intentional acts, whether of commission or omission. If a person has for-gotten to fulfil a duty, it is aimless to inquire about his reason for forgetting; there is no *motive*[1] for forgetfulness or inadvertence or error, though such things may be judged culpable on the score that it was within the agent's power and control to remember, advert to, or inform himself of, his duty. We have seen that motive-inquiries are in place even when the agent has not explicitly formulated his reason for acting; but it is at least necessary that he should have done the action with some reason or purpose in view, albeit only implicitly, if a motive is to be ascribed to him.

(ii) *Criteria of motive-statements*

So much for the conditions necessary if an act is to be a candidate for motive-investigation. Next we must inquire into the criteria by which we may identify motive-statements. Bentham, after the preliminary loose definition of Motive which we have criticized, gives the following more precise definition of what constitutes a Motive in the sense relevant to morals:

The motives with which alone we have any concern, are such as are of a nature to act upon the will. By a motive then, in this sense of the word, is to be understood any thing whatsoever, which, by influencing the will of a sensitive being, is supposed to serve as a means of determining him to act, or voluntarily to forbear to act, upon any occasion.[2]

Such a definition successfully draws attention to the fact that a motive-statement always, to some extent at least, reveals

[1] i.e. in any more than the psychologist's sense of an 'unconscious motive'. [2] p. 98.

the reason why the agent acted and so has the force of explaining his action. Unfortunately, however, the definition
is verified in many things that are not motives. Many
answers to the question, 'Why did you do X?' are motive-
statements: e.g. 'I needed the money', 'To win votes'; but
many others are not: e.g. 'I felt bored', 'I am a free-trader',
'He asked me', 'BOAC are using jets on that flight', 'In
British politics, breakaway parties always fizzle out'—such
statements may serve, on various occasions, as explanations,
or as reasons for a person's action, but they are not in
ordinary terminology motive-statements. This definition,
then, lets in many things that do not count at motives; but
it might well serve as a rough definition of a much more
extensive term: explanations. There are four different types
of explanation to which Bentham's definition may apply.

1. It applies to the type of statements that give as an
explanation of the act in question some event external to the
agent; but these are not motive-statements. Bentham's own
example is a case in point: 'the coming up of a lottery ticket,
by which money devolves to you' may very well 'influence the
will' of the winner and 'serve as a means of determining him
to act': say, to take a trip overseas. The statement, 'He won
the pools', would be quite an appropriate answer to the
question, 'Why is Jones going to Honolulu?', but not to the
question, 'What is Jones's motive for going to Honolulu?'
Two qualifications, however, need to be made here. First,
the mentioning of an external event, though not a motive-
statement, may often give the *grounds* for the agent's motive.
It may be known or suspected that a person's action was
motivated by fear, or gratitude, or compassion, and the explanation may be given by telling of some external event
which gave rise to such motives: thus the question, 'Why did
you give money to Smith?' may be answered by any of the
following statements: 'He had a gun'; 'He once saved my
life'; 'He was put off work a month ago and his wife has just

had a baby'. These are not motive-statements, but they often make clear the grounds of the motive we suspected. Second, such replies may be idiomatic expressions which are rhetorical or self-depreciatory shorthand for, or paraphrases of, some other proposition which *is* a motive-statement; instead of saying that my motive was generosity or gratitude or fear I may use one of the above references to an external incident.

2. Many sorts of explanation may be roughly collected under the heading 'beliefs'. This open-texture expression is meant to cover all sorts of principles and rules which are chosen, or at least accepted, as guides to decisions and actions. We may explain a person's having refused a certain dish by referring to the fact that he is a Catholic or a Jew or a Hindu, or a vegetarian, or a supporter of a political boycott. Here again such things may often show the *grounds* of a person's motive, and it will be frequently possible to use them as a key point in a fuller explanation which *is* a motive-statement: e.g. he believes that the South African Government will abandon its policy of *apartheid* if strong, organized economic pressure is brought to bear on it; he wants to do all he can for the abolition of *apartheid*, and believes that this boycott can apply the necessary pressure; hence his refusal. The loose word 'beliefs' embraces another type of explanation. It need not refer solely to abiding matters of principle or creed; on a given occasion a man's knowledge (or ignorance) of a relevant fact, or his personal judgement about the means best calculated to secure a given end, may well 'serve as a means determining him to act' as he does, or to act later rather than sooner. The fact that the Allies believed that the Dardanelles were heavily mined explains why they postponed the Gallipoli landing from November 1914 until the next April; but that mistaken belief was not the *motive* for the delay, or for the subsequent landing.

3. A third type of explanation is given in terms of various

non-objective-seeking drives, impulses, and so on, by which
human beings are visited. Many of these are emotions induced by a particular occasion. Excitement can cause a usually
cautious batsman to swish foolishly at the first ball he receives
in a big match; nervousness often afflicts a person being
examined for a driving licence, and leads to his making mistakes which he would normally avoid; embarrassment can
cause an habitually eloquent person to dry up completely;
a mother who fears that her child has been lost or hurt on
suddenly finding him unharmed may storm at him in rebuke,
or embrace him, or cry. We might then explain the behaviour
of such persons in terms of excitement, nervousness, embarrassment, or relief. Such visitations may be sudden and strong,
though they are not objective-seeking. But often explanations
coming under this heading refer, not to episodic emotions
induced by a particular occasion, but to things less transient.
A mood of boredom induced by a wet Sunday afternoon may
move a middle-aged person to go to bed or a group of youths
to steal a car; a similar though more deep-seated dissatisfaction, too permanent to be called a mood, may lead a girl
of a wealthy family to join the Red Cross or edit a left-wing
magazine. There are traits of character or disposition more
deeply rooted still, such as sloth or the more settled sorts of
self-pity or diffidence, which also seem to belong in this
category. Any of these things, then, may explain, or help to
explain, actions, and Bentham's definition of motive is
verified in each of them; for it is nervousness or excitement
or diffidence or the rest that, visiting the agent, 'serve as
a means of determining him to act' upon a given occasion;
but they are not motives, and the explanations in which they
appear are not motive-explanations.

   4. Finally, we come to statements which explain a person's
action in terms of its, or his, objective; and it is within this
range that motive-statements are located. What is the criterion which marks off motive-statements from others within

this range? We may notice two remarks in this connexion which seem to contrast with each other.

Peters, though recalling that psychoanalysts have often seemed to discredit our actions by unearthing our motives, points out that in ordinary life we seek or ascribe motives only 'when a breach with an established expectation has occurred and there is need to *justify* some action'.[1] One might add that there are cases when the presence of a motive (in some sense of the word) may not justify, but may excuse a person's behaviour, or at least mitigate his guilt. On the other hand, Nowell-Smith remarks that, in ordinary life, to ask what someone's motive in doing something was is usually to imply that the motive was a disreputable one: thus one might say, 'Oh, I know he's very faithful about visiting his rich aunt since she had a stroke; but what do you think is his motive?'; or, 'He took no interest in his constituents when Barchester was a blue-riband seat; why do you think he's suddenly become so attentive since the redistribution?' The two approaches seem to be at odds: Peters seems to be saying that a motive usually justifies a bad action, Nowell-Smith that it vitiates a good one.

Some attempt such as the following might be made to embrace these two apparently opposed propositions in a single broader one: It seems that we usually ascribe M as the motive of the action A only when M and A belong to different moral genera or species. (1) We do so when we believe that an apparently good action was prompted by an unworthy motive. To have a strong desire, inclination, or temptation to do murder, and then to refuse oneself a ready opportunity, seems to be a praiseworthy forbearance, or at least a morally good and dutiful decision. But in Hamlet's case it was thoroughly base, for it was prompted by a motive more wicked than that of inflicting death on his uncle; he resolved to wait until he could catch him about some act that had no

[1] 'Motives and Motivation', *Philosophy*, April 1956, p. 118.

relish of salvation in it, and send his soul to hell. (2) We also
do so when, by attributing some good motive to a person who
has apparently done wrong, we justify or excuse his action,
or at least mitigate his guilt. The breaking of an appointment
may be justified if a man's motive is the performance of some
urgent act of charity, excused if it is concern about his health,
mitigated if it is a business opportunity of slightly greater
value than the appointment involves. (3) It is also often
appropriate to say that M is the motive of the action A when
M and A belong to different moral species: both are good or
both bad, but the motive causes the episode to fall under
a different species of goodness or badness than the action
alone would have done. If a woman commits adultery for the
sake of money, or a man in the hope of eliciting some commercial or political or military secret about his paramour's
husband, we may well cast about for the apt characterization
of this 'ulterior' motive. But where there is adultery solely
'at the bidding of appetite', as Aristotle says, we do not say
that the motive was lust, or sexual desire. The apparent
exception to this is not, I think, a real one; we sometimes say,
'His motive for doing the action A was simply and solely M',
where M is something necessarily or naturally associated
with A; for instance, his reason for giving money to the
beggar was simply to alleviate misery, his motive nothing but
generosity. Such a remark will be made typically when someone has been inclined to suspect that there is some reason
other than the obvious one for the deed in question, and the
phrase 'simply and solely' is intended to dispel the suspicion; it is an emphatic way of denying that there is an
'ulterior' motive to seek. The presence of some such phrase
as 'simply and solely' draws attention to the fact that we are
making use of the expression in some emphatic or slightly
abnormal way. It is not quite comfortable to say that the
desire of money is the motive of a theft, as Bentham does,
or that benevolence is the motive of an act of kindness.

Frequently, then, a motive and the action which it prompts belong to different moral baskets.

However, even this point, which brings together the points made by Peters and Nowell-Smith, is not sufficiently extensive to fit all the facts; it is only a special case of something more general, which is not restricted to moral contexts at all. A motive-statement usually has the force of an explanation. Now explanations are advanced or looked for especially when there is something unusual on hand. We are therefore inclined to ask for an explanation in terms of motive only when confronted with an action which is in some way unusual, or when we suspect that a normal action was done for some unusual reason; and we are inclined to ascribe a motive either to dispel the misconception that the usual reason for a given action is at work, or to dispel the suspicion that it is not. Normally, to ask why Jones helped the blind man across the street is pointless, because the normal reason is built into 'helped . . . blind'. *A fortiori*, 'He stole that because he wanted it' is pointless, since 'wanting' is already built into 'stealing'. So we ask, or say, 'Why' only when there is, or may be, a peculiar reason: something not built into the act-term: something, therefore, 'ulterior' to it. Many of our regular act-terms already connote the reasons for making the arm- or leg-movements, or tongue-movements: compare, 'Why is he planting potatoes?' with 'Why is he dropping those things into holes in the ground?' The standard or normal reason for doing something is not a motive, then, although Bentham constantly offers it as one; he says, for instance, that the motive of a man who commits rape is the same as the motive of the man who exercises the rights of marriage with his wife: sexual desire. A likely sign that M is not the motive of the action X will be the response, 'But *of course* M was his reason for doing X.' One does not explain an action by mentioning something which is already known as its natural associate.

It is therefore inappropriate to say that Q is a person's motive for doing the action X, not only when they belong to the same moral genus or species, but also when they are naturally and normally associated, as may occur in three ways. It may be that Q is the natural general *description* of several activities or undertakings, one of which is X: to say that one's reason for teaching a boy Latin is to further his education is not to give one's motive for doing it; but to say that it is to ingratiate oneself with his family is to do so. It may be that Q is the natural *accompaniment* of X: the pleasure of slaking one's thirst is not one's motive for drinking, but the prospect of clinching a contract with one's drinking-companion may be. Most important, it is inappropriate to say that Q is a person's motive for doing X when Q is the natural *objective* or result of the action X: to say that an undergraduate is taking Schools in order to obtain a degree, or that a person shot a testator in order to kill him, or that the Government is creating work in a distressed area to provide jobs for the unemployed, is not to give the motives that prompted these actions; but one could say quite properly that the under-graduate's motive was to please his parents, or the heir's to inherit his bequest, or the Government's to attract votes in a marginal seat. 'War's very object is victory', said Mac-Arthur: its object, but not its motive.

Nowell-Smith remarks with approval that Aristotle would have said that the *for the sake of* clause is part of the essence of every motive.[1] I think that he should have said 'of the essence of every motive-explanation'; but the remark sums up much of what has just been said. On the one hand, the phrase *for the sake of* indicates that an explanation is being given in terms of the agent's objective; and this is a feature of motive-statements. On the other hand, we do not say that a person did the action A for the sake of X if X is the natural description of accompaniment or objective of A, unless we

[1] *Ethics*, p. 126.

wish to dispel a mistaken suspicion or misconception; and this distinguishes motive-statements from other explanations given in terms of objective.

(iii) *Types of motive-statement*

However, Nowell-Smith does not seem to have noticed the ambiguity of the phrase 'for the sake of'. Consider such phrases as: 'for the sake of Abraham our father (who *was* your friend)'; 'for the sake of gratitude, or friendship'; 'for the sake of the children (who *will* suffer')'; 'for the sake of decency, or if that won't move you, at least for the sake of appearances'; 'for conscience' sake'; 'for duty's sake'. Such examples suggest that it is misleading to speak of the phrase 'for the sake of' as if it were a univocal term, or as if it were simply *the* criterion of another univocal term, Motive. Even before we begin to study the logic of motive-statements we can distinguish three distinct usages of 'Motive', three distinct types of objective-giving explanation introduced by the phrase 'for the sake of'.

First there is the forward-looking sense of motive; the agent's motive is given as his end or goal; his objective lies in the future, beyond the objective naturally associated with such an action, and he is said to act *for the sake of* that ulterior objective. In this sense the phrase 'for the sake of' will often be used with a gerund of producing, achieving, obtaining, employing, or experiencing, and often with some general term descriptive of the end in view, e.g. praise, prestige, profit. Perhaps the best term for this is 'intended consequences': 'intended', to indicate the directedness of the action; 'consequences', to indicate something lying beyond, not contained in, the act under its natural description. It is interesting to remark that Bentham considered the word *inducement* 'in its signification more comprehensive than the word *motive*, and on some occasions more apposite' (p. 97, n. 1). Yet surely it is only this sense of the word motive—viz.

end or goal—to which 'inducement' corresponds, and even with
this it is not synonymous; an inducement is rather something
put forward by another person in the hope of the agent's acting
upon it as a motive. An inducement is not necessarily efficacious;
a motive, in this first sense, is. At all events, a motive in this
sense lies in the future with regard to the action it motivates.

A second usage of Motive is backward-looking; the action
is said to be done for the sake of some past fact, action, or
experience: as when the motive is gratitude or revenge. This
often has the character of repaying a debt or redressing an
imbalance. In practice it is not always easy to separate this
sense from the first. Thus, a new Head of Department intro-
duces new policies or extends patronage to new assistants;
Department gossips are divided as to whether his motive
is to show his contempt for the previous head, to earn
a reputation for progressive thought, or to reassure himself
of his own authority. Not many human actions, perhaps,
are prompted by one single motive, and some people have
thought that all actions have at least some element of forward-
looking motivation; nevertheless past-directedness *is* a feature
of some motives, where something now past is felt as giving
rise to present action. One must look carefully at such cases:
sometimes, although the past fact may be the antecedent
condition, some future emotion or experience may be the
aim or purpose—the satisfaction of showing that 'Now I am
Caesar', or of seeing one's enemy silenced or humiliated
(Evelyn Waugh speaks of the warm glow in the hearts of old
men who hear of their contemporaries' misfortunes). But
one cannot reduce *all* such past-prompted motives to the
desire for future satisfactions. Gratitude may urge something
that is exacting, dull, and unrewarding, which sometimes will
be necessarily unknown and unacknowledged by the beneficiary; but it is unreal to say that one always performs acts
of gratitude for the sake of enjoying the nice feeling that
being grateful engenders.

There is a third type of motive-statement to which we have already adverted: that in which the context of discussion moves us to insist that the objective in question was simply and solely something naturally associated with the act in question. Such a statement is made typically in order to dispel the misconception or suspicion that the agent was prompted by an 'ulterior motive', and denies that his objective was anything other than the natural accompaniment, objective, or outcome of such actions. To say that the motive for an act of kindness was 'nothing but benevolence' is not to add something to the account of the performance, but simply to dispel the suspicion that it was done with any end in view beyond its obvious purpose or result—the relief of pain or poverty or loneliness. To say that an act of meanness had avarice for its motive is not to tell us something further about the miser, but simply to forestall the possible misconception that he may have had some good end in view which might have justified his parsimony, or even some more colourful bad end which might have faintly redeemed it as a little more human and excusable. In this sense a motive-statement will often be made by saying that the action X was done 'simply and solely for the sake of Q', where Q is the accepted standard reason for doing X; or by saying that it was done 'simply *for its own sake*'.

One final point. In each of the three types of motive-statement just distinguished, the motive-phrase may be either a general term, describing a type or kind of motives; or it may be a particular instance of one such type. Thus, as an example of the first type, it could be said that a murder had been done for the sake of *profit*, or in order to steal the victim's wallet; of the second type, that A had made a gift to B out of *gratitude*, or because B had saved his life; of the third, that a man has been faithfully visiting his sick rich aunt simply out of *compassion*, or simply because he feels sorry for her not receiving many visitors. The general term need not be a single word, like gratitude, revenge, or compassion; it may be a phrase. Instead of the single word 'vainglory' Christ uses the motive-phrase 'in order to be seen by men'; nowadays the phrase 'keeping up with the Joneses' is often used to indicate the motive, 'emulation'. Even when such phrases have the appearance of concreteness and particularity, they are often indeed class-phrases under which a great number of single instances may be subsumed.

§ 2. THE LOGIC OF MOTIVE-STATEMENTS

My purpose here is not, of course, to pretend to put forward a complete account of the logic of motive-statements, but to advert to a number of points about it which clear the ground for considering the morality of motives. To this end it will be helpful to review briefly, in the light of the above linguistic investigation, a number of points philosophers have made, and then proceed to my own account.

Bentham wants to distinguish 'two kinds of objects' denoted by the word motive. The first are those

really existing incidents from whence the act in question is supposed to take its rise. . . . They may be either, 1. The *internal* perception of any individual lot of pleasure or pain, the expectation of which is looked upon as calculated to determine you to act in such and such a manner. . . . or, 2. Any *external* event, the happening whereof is regarded as having a tendency to bring about the perception of such pleasure or such pain.

The second kind of motive-object, he says, is

a certain fictitious entity, a passion, an affection of the mind, an ideal being which upon the happening of any such incident is considered as operating upon the mind, and prompting it to take its course. Motives of this class are Avarice, Indolence, Benevolence and so forth.[1]

[1] pp. 98–99.

In the light of what has already been said, such an account seems to be unsatisfactory on four scores.

First, it was suggested above that external events are not motives, though they are often the ground of a motive: the person's motive is, say, the desire of X; and mention of the external event shows why he finds X desirable.

Next, motive-words such as Avarice and Benevolence, whether written with a large initial letter or small, need not be thought of as labels on different little machines within the agent, from which acts of the relevant labelled type duly emerge. There is no need to accord them any mysterious status at all; they are simply class-words, general terms of which an individual avaricious or benevolent act is a particular instance, as an individual act of killing is a particular instance of the general term Homicide. Furthermore, it is strange to put Avarice, Indolence, and Benevolence in one motive-basket. Indolence is not a motive-word at all: my indolence may *explain* my failure to do my duty, or even, perhaps, characterize it: but it is not my *motive* for failing. Benevolence and Avarice, we have seen, may often be called motives in the third sense discussed above, namely they may deny that the agent has any end in view beyond the obvious and natural outcome of his action. On the other hand, such words as Avarice, or Ambition, may often be general descriptions of ends or aims more or less secret: an act thought to have been done in the public weal looks very different if it is shown to have been done for some selfish end—boosting a bank balance or winning political power. Such words, then, are ascribing a motive in the first sense described above, though subsuming it under a general heading instead of describing it in detail.

Third, Bentham's hedonistic psychology leads him to restrict effective motives to 'the internal perception of an individual lot of pleasure or pain' which the agent desires to enjoy or avoid in the future. Of course, this quite well

describes a very common motive-situation. But it is not true
of many others. Gratitude, it was suggested above, may
urge me to undertake a task that is exacting, dull, and unrewarding, which sometimes will necessarily be unknown or
unacknowledged by the beneficiary; and it is unreal to say
that one always performs acts of gratitude in order to enjoy
the nice feeling that being grateful engenders—'because it
makes you feel good'.

Finally, Bentham's account presupposes his usual para-
mechanical picture of action: motive generates intention,
which produces action, just as the hammer explodes the
cartridge, which fires the bullet. Enough has been said elsewhere about the general defects of this theory, and the particular aspect of it which deals with motive has been attacked,
successfully as it seems to me, by Ryle.

Ryle has not criticized Bentham specifically, but the whole
idea that motives are acts or states or feelings, happenings
or occurrences.[1] Ryle says that a man who acts out of vanity
is not a man who had a feeling of vanity immediately before
he acted. He argues that motives are rather propensities,
trends of behaviour, or traits of character, and hence that
motive-explanations are logically akin to disposition-explana-
tions, which he holds to be 'law-like hypothetical propositions'. Thus, if it is asked why the window broke, two
answers are possible: one, that someone threw a stone
through it; the other, that glass is brittle. The first is an
occurrence-explanation, which Bentham, as we have seen,
considers to be one sort of motive-statement; the second
a disposition-explanation, called by Ryle a 'law-like hypothetical proposition', since it may be translated, 'Glass, if
sharply struck or twisted, would not dissolve or stretch, but
fly into fragments.' For Ryle, motive-explanations are of this
second, dispositional, type: 'to explain an action as done from
a certain motive is not to correlate it with an occult cause,

[1] *Concept of Mind* (London, 1949), c. IV.

but to subsume it under a propensity or behaviour-trend';
'Aristotle realized that in talking about motives we are talking
about dispositions of a certain sort'. Ryle has chosen two
examples, however, that leave him open to criticism.

The first is patriotism. Where it is said that the motive for
a man's action is patriotism, Ryle denies (1) that such an
explanation necessarily refers to *feelings* of patriotism, and
(2) that these feelings are to be construed as internal prods
causing him to behave as he does; instead, (3) he asserts that
it is to point to a disposition or propensity in the man which
leads to his doing certain sorts of action when his country
is in need or difficulty. Nowell-Smith has criticized this account: a man may always do the patriotic thing, he may
have the disposition or propensity which means that *if*
a national crisis arose he *would* always do what his country
needed; but, he says,

it is still open to us to ask what was his motive for so acting. His
actions are quite consistent with his wanting to gain kudos or his
having his eye on the post-war political scene; and they are also
consistent with his wanting to help his country.[1]

Yet it is only in the latter case that we say that the man's
motives are patriotic, or that patriotism was his motive. The
test of his motive is not, 'What did he do?' nor, 'Was he
always likely to do it?' but, 'For the sake of what did he do
it?' Ryle's other example is hardly more fortunate: 'He
boasted from vanity.' Mrs. Foot has written about it: 'Considered as a statement assigning a motive to a particular
action it would be uninformative, for except in very special
cases *boasting is* acting out of vanity.'[2]

Nowell-Smith's criticism seems sound as far as it goes;
but I suggest that it fails to take account of the three different

[1] p. 126.
[2] 'Free will as Involving Determinism', in *Philosophical Review*, Oct.
1957, p. 446.

senses of motive covered by the phrase 'for the sake of', and applies to only one of them. The case of 'Patriotism', as Ryle and Nowell-Smith use it, is an instance of the third sense: what is being said is (1) this is the sort of action calculated to promote the welfare of the agent's country, and (2) what he hopes to achieve by it is nothing but his country's good—not his own financial gain, nor political advancement, nor the good of his family or party or class. A motive-statement of this sort denies the existence of an end ulterior to, not naturally connected with, the action, and subsumes it under some general descriptive word. Nowell-Smith seems to be successful in criticizing Ryle's account of this sense of Motive; but neither he nor Ryle accounts satisfactorily for the other senses of the term: senses which are, I think, more important. Think of the backward-looking sense of motive, e.g. gratitude or revenge. How can Ryle's disposition-theory explain the fact that the very same person, with the very same reason for being grateful or vengeful, will act on different occasions now gratefully, now ungratefully; now vengefully, now not? Given the same conditions of temperature, sharpness, hardness, speed and angle of impact, and so on, a stone will always break a given window; the would-if model works very nicely. But this is not true of a human being presented with opportunites for gratitude or revenge.

Moreover, the forward-looking sense of Motive appears to have been neglected completely: that which gives the aim or end or purpose of an action; and a similar objection would tell against the attempt to reduce such motive-statements to law-like propositions. It may be said that, on a given occasion, a man's motive was political advancement, or monetary gain, or the fear of hell, or the desire for heaven; but an account of this in terms of would-if involves saying that the next time, and any time, that the same situation arises the person will act in the same way. It seems to entail that a person never acts out of character: a man whose conduct is usually prompted or shaped by motives of gain can never act unselfishly on an individual occasion. 'If p, then q' licenses the inference, 'But p, therefore q'.

Furthermore, Ryle's account fits only cases where the motive is given as a general word or phrase. But we have found that motive-statements, in all three senses, can be given in quite concrete terms. One might say, in a discussion on the morality of suicide, 'It is true that Oates walked out to his death in the snow; but his motive was to relieve his companions of the dangerous burden of an injured man.' How does this bear out Ryle's thesis, 'The imputation of a motive for a particular action is not a causal inference to an un-witnessed event, but the subsumption of an episode-proposition under a law-like proposition'?

Let us pause here to summarize what has so far emerged about motive-statements. Although some points made by philosophers seem to be unsatisfactory, five points do appear to have been established. First, when it is said, 'A's motive for doing the action X was M', we do not mean that M was some item of A's mental furniture: an emotion, or mood, or disposition, or trait. It is not that motives are a certain kind of thing; rather, motive-statements are a certain kind of statement, viz. explanations. Second, not every explanation of A's doing X is a motive-statement: the question, 'How do you explain A's having done X?' could receive such answers as, 'He was angry, or bored', 'He's a free-trader', 'He was starved of affection as a child'; but these are not motive-statements; only explanations in terms of reasons are motive-statements. Third, not every reason-giving explanation is a motive-statement; 'His reason for doing X was M' usually is; 'The reason for his doing X was Q' frequently is not: e.g. 'That's the sort of example he always received at home', 'All the Emsworths inherit that pig-headed strain'. Fourth, a point which rather overlaps with the second, above: not every answer to the question, 'What was A's reason for doing

X?' is a motive-statement. This is frequently the case where the answers refer to the agent's beliefs, often mistaken, about tactical or technical facts, e.g. 'What was his reason for delaying the attack?' 'He thought the fort was fully defended'; 'What was his reason for going by Comet?' 'He thinks the Boeings are unsafe'. Explanations in terms of A's-reason-for-doing-X are motive-statements only when they shed light on his *objective*. Fifth, the objective may be given as a general term or phrase, or as a concrete, individual instance.

To this extent, then, Nowell-Smith seems to be right in agreeing that Aristotle's ἕνεκα, 'for the sake of', is essential to every motive-statement. So far so good. But more has to be said before we have a sufficient account of the logic of motive-statements to be able to study the morality of motives. We have found that there are three different usages of the word 'motive'; are these simply linguistically distinct, and capable of being lumped into one logical basket? I think that they are not; and I suggest that it is a mistake to think of the phrase 'for the sake of' as logically univocal, occurring in usages only chronologically distinct (forward-looking, backward-looking). Macbeth's motive for murder was of the first sense: it was a future end to which Duncan's death was a means. Hamlet's murder of his uncle had a different motive: it was to redress an injustice committed in the past. Each gives the agent's reason for acting in terms of his objective, and can be characterized in a single word: ambition, or revenge. But this should not make us think that each has the same logic.

The logic of the first, forward-looking, type of motive-statement is clear enough. It is of the means-end pattern; in this sense, to say 'A's motive for performing the action X was M' is equivalent to saying 'The end A wanted was M, and he did X because it was a means promising to attain M'. There is no mystery as to why A should have M as an objective; the end given is usually something which is a common human objective—say pleasure, or prestige, or profit; the motive-statement thus explains X in terms of objective, simply by showing that doing X can be expected to lead to getting M, and no explanation is needed of why one seeks M.

The second type of motive-statement, characterized so far as backward-looking, gives quite a different sort of explanation-in-terms-of-objective. For one thing, the objective is not some consequence that lies beyond the action, but is either identified or naturally associated with it. Furthermore, the objective is not something which seems, without some special reason, a likely objective of action. Revenge may be pleasurable, as the narrator found in Poe's *Cask of Amontillado*, or as Stalin is quoted as saying: 'To mark your victim, to plan minutely, to have your revenge, and then to go to bed: there is nothing sweeter in the world'; but it need not be attractive for its own sake, or enjoyable in prospect, as Hamlet seems to exemplify. This is even clearer in the case of gratitude: an observer asks himself why the agent should have undertaken a task which he finds costly, or painful, or boring, and holds no promise of reward; the explanation in terms of gratitude answers the question. Here, then, is the function of motive-statements of this second sort: they explain that this objective, not of itself attractive or desirable or a likely human target in the normal course of events, is thought worthy of pursuit because of special circumstances created in the past.

Are gratitude and revenge the only motives of this kind? It is true that there are other backward-looking *reasons-for-acting*: I am waiting here now because I promised to do so; I am driving with unusual care today because I was fined last week; character traits of sarcasm, scepticism, and food faddism are explained by Freud in terms of unusually great oral delights in infancy. Some of these are only 'the reason for his doing X', but some of them are indeed 'his reason for doing X'. But none of them is a motive-statement: they are not explanation in terms of objective; Aristotle's ἕνεκα is missing. One might be tempted to think that, once an explanation is given in terms of an objective thought to be worthy of pursuit because of special circumstances created in the past, the motive revealed will always be either gratitude or revenge, or a species or instance of one or the other. For whatever it was in the past which affects me here and now will either have been good or bad: if my action now is prompted by the memory of something good done to me in the past, my motive is called gratitude; if by something bad, it is called revenge. Indeed, may this not suggest a simpler account of the logic of such motive-statements? namely, that they explain the agent's action in terms of his desire to redress some imbalance. They will always include an element of 'paying back', not necessarily in the sense of meeting an obligation in justice, but in the sense of *matching* the objective of my action with the ground of my motive: in the case of gratitude, the ground of my motive is a past good done to the present agent by the present recipient, so the objective of the action is a present good done by the present agent to the present recipient; in the case of revenge, some past evil or hurt is to be matched with a similar one now.

And yet, have we quite reached the crux? One not only wonders whether gratitude and revenge completely divide motive-statements of the second sense; one wonders whether 'forward-looking' and 'backward-looking' divide all motive-statements, other than those of the third sense (which merely deny the existence of any motive beyond the natural associate of the action). Macbeth's motive for killing Duncan looks forward; Hamlet's for killing his uncle looks back; but what of Othello's motive? He does not hope to gain by Desdemona's death; and his action is prompted, not by something in the past, but by something (as he thinks) taking place at present. Jealousy and love are two motives for which our account has so far failed to provide. They are extremely important 'drives by which human beings are visited'; they commonly *explain* human action, and do so in terms of its objective; they are not, at least necessarily, to be reduced to forward-looking or backward-looking. Yet it would do violence to ordinary language to deny that love and jealousy are common human motives. Are we to postulate a fourth sense of motive, or a fourth type of motive-statements?

I think not. The essential point in motive-statements of the second sense seems to be, not that they look back to a ground which lies in the past: but that they explain why a particular course of action, which has no intrinsic attractiveness, has been in some way rendered an objective worthy of pursuit by some circumstance *not naturally or necessarily connected with it*. This circumstance may lie in the past, of course; but a present circumstance may also play exactly the same role. Why does a person do things that are boring, or distasteful, or thankless, or dangerous? Often because of his love of the beneficiary; the love of a friend may explain a person's seeking the most unattractive of all human objectives, namely, laying down his life for him. Jealousy may function in the same way, leading a person to decide on a course of action which gives no pleasure in its performance, and only bitterness in its consequences: as in the case of Othello. Similarly, it is often accurate to say that a person's motive was 'a sense of duty', or that he acted 'for conscience' sake'; and these also are motive-explanations of the second type. For they explain why a person does X: not because doing-X gives pleasure or is in any way attractive for its own sake, nor as a means to some end which is pleasurable or attractive: but for the extrinsic reason that it is required by duty, or enjoined by conscience. Such motive-statements explain, then, why a particular objective, which at first sight seems an unpromising target for human action, has come to be thought worthy of pursuit: they reveal the presence of some external circumstance which moves a man to decide on a course of action which he would not choose for its own intrinsic pleasurableness or worth, nor for its consequences.

Motive-statements of the third sort are much less entitled to the name; for their function is to dispel the suspicion or correct the misconception that the agent had any end in view other than that which is naturally associated with the act. This may be done by mentioning emphatically the general word or term of which the act is held to be an instance, as when one says, 'No, he didn't hope to gain anything by the gift; his motive was generosity, pure and simple'; or it may be done by giving what is practically an alternative description of the act, stressing the aspect under which the natural accompaniment or outcome of the act is pursued: for instance, 'Why did you give him money?': 'Just because I felt sorry for him, that's all.' It was suggested above that it is not quite appropriate to say that M is a person's motive for doing X when M is a natural or normal associate of X, whether as its natural description, accompaniment, or objective. At that rate, motives of this third class are not quite strictly motives; and explanations of this sort are motive-statements only in the sense that they repudiate the suggestion or allay the suspicion that any ('ulterior') motive is present. Aristotle's ἕνεκα is in place here only in the sense that one says that the agent did X 'simply *for its own sake*'.

Some of these points may be seen a little more clearly if, in the light of them, we read Dewey and Tufts's account of the distinction between Intention and Motive:

Intention is *what* a man means to do; motive is the personal frame of mind which indicates *why* he means to do it. Intention is the concrete aim or purpose: the results which are foreseen and wanted. Motive is the state of mind which renders these consequences, rather than others, interesting and attractive.[1]

The following remarks suggest themselves. (1) It would have been better to say that an intention-statement tells us what a

[1] J. Dewey and J. H. Tufts, *Ethics* (New York, 1914), p. 247.

man means to do, or what his concrete aim and purpose is, rather than saying that these are what his intention *is*; intention and motive are not two separate pieces of mental furniture: rather, intention-statements are commonly identificatory and motive-statements explanatory. (2) Motive-in-the-first-sense does not 'render the consequences of an act attractive'; profit, prestige, and pleasure and the like are naturally attractive consequences of acting, and are not rendered so by some personal frame of mind. Rather, motive-statements of the first sort explain why a person decides on a certain act: because he expects it to lead to one of those attractive consequences. (3) The last sentence in the quotation partly accounts for motives of the second type, at least to this extent: that motive-statements are often called for to explain why a person has done something which is neither interesting nor attractive. (4) However, motives-in-the-second-sense do not always render the act which they prompt interesting, or attractive; the act may still be boring, or distasteful, or—as in Oates's case—much worse. All that is needed is that, as the first sentence in the quotation says, the motive-statement indicate why the agent decides to do it. (5) It is curious, too, to see how Dewey and Tufts run together what-a-man-means-to-do, and results or consequences. We have seen that it is commonly possible to draw a line, though not always a fixed line, between 'act' and 'consequences'. Given that distinction, (*a*) Intention may refer to the act itself, and motive (in the first sense) to the consequences; (*b*) the 'concrete aim or purpose' may be intended to *produce* 'the results which are foreseen and wanted', and thus not to be identifiable with them; (*c*) motive, or more properly a motive-statement (in the third sense), may refer to the act itself, and deny a reference to consequences.

Let us sum up. All motive-statements are (1) explanations (2) in terms of the agent's objective; hence the phrase, 'for the sake of', or something with equivalent force, is essential to every motive-statement. But this is verified in three different ways. In the first case one says, 'What I really want is not the natural accompaniment or outcome of the act X, but the end M to which X is simply a means. I do X for the sake of M.' In the second sense one says, 'What I want is indeed the natural outcome or accompaniment of the action; but I want it, not because of its intrinsic attractiveness, but because of its being made worth while by some extrinsic circumstance C. I do X because of C.' In the third sense one says, 'What I want is simply and solely the natural outcome of X, which I want simply for its own sake.'

§ 3. THE EFFECT OF MOTIVE ON MORALITY

It remains to seek some of the rules concerning the effect of the agent's motive on the moral value of his performance, and I propose to restrict the discussion to motives in the first sense. For, on the one hand, motives in the third sense do not, of course, make any difference to an act's morality; rather, motive-statements of the third sort deny the presence of a motive which would do so. Motives in the second sense, on the other hand, affect the morality of the acts which they prompt in many different ways; separate essays would have to be written to examine the different effects of, say, envy, anger, and revenge; love; the sense of duty; and the promptings of conscience. But it is possible to gather under general headings the main points concerning the effect of motives in the first sense on the morality of the performance of which they form part; and that is the aim of this final section.

We shall here be taking for granted the thesis, proposed in Chapter 1, that there are certain kinds of act which can be distinguished from their consequences; for motives in the first sense stand to the act which they prompt as ends stand to means, or as intended consequences to the acts which produce them. Now Bentham remarks: 'The case is, that from one and the same motive, and from every kind of motive, may proceed actions that are good, others that are bad, and others that are indifferent.'[1] This suggests the headings for our discussion; we shall work through the various combinations of good motives and bad ones with acts which are (*a*) indifferent; (*b*) good; (*c*) bad. A final question will consider what Bentham calls 'obliquely intended consequences'.

There are two preliminary points to be made. First, in many cases it is necessary to distinguish whether the end in question is the agent's total or partial motive. One may say that M is a person's *total* motive for doing the act X if he simply would not do X were he not to attain M by doing so; he does X solely for the sake of M, and not at all for its own sake: nor for the sake of any other, allied, consequence. M may be called his *partial* motive for doing X in either of two cases. In the first, he does indeed hope to attain M by the performance, but none the less would do it even if he had no such hope; he does X for the sake of M, indeed, but also partly for its own sake: for example, he visits an ailing aunt in the hope that this may win him a place in her will; but even were he to find that she had lost her fortune, he would continue to visit her out of compassion: the act of kindness is not *merely* a means to his end. In the second case, the agent hopes to attain two ends, M and M'; for instance, he hopes that his research will lead to the discovery of a cure for leukaemia, and also that it may win a Nobel Prize: but even if he were to learn that, for some reason, he would not be eligible for the prize, he would continue with his research; the act is indeed done for the sake of M, although not only for its sake. It seems happier to account in these terms for the doctor who treats a patient and expects a fee for it, than in terms of Socrates' distinction between the doctor-*qua*-doctor and the doctor-*qua*-wage-earner.

Second, many examples of motive are cases of doing-X in

order to avoid the consequences of not-doing-X: from
mowing one's lawn in order not to be criticized by one's neighbours, to forging a cheque in order not to have one's defalca-
tions discovered. There is no need to spell out separately the
effects of such motives in the different possible cases of their
occurrence; the same rules will govern their moral appraisal
as apply to the other cases we must consider: is (1) the act
itself, and (2) the motive, (a) indifferent, (b) good, (c) bad?

(i) *Effect on indifferent acts*

First, there are performances in which the act itself is
morally indifferent. When a person's motive for performing
such an act is a morally good one, it renders the act itself
a morally good one. For instance, driving a car is of itself
morally indifferent; but an arduous drive undertaken to take
a doctor or nurse to the help of a sick or injured person will
often be commendable. It is not only that part of the performance which is obviously admirable, viz. the treatment of
the injury or the alleviation of suffering, which is held to be
good, but also that part which is of itself indifferent, viz. the
drive. For the person who drives the car may be different
from the person who treats the injury; he may not even leave
the car to see the patient, but hurry on to another engagement,
or shy away from the sight of blood; none the less his con-
tribution will itself deserve gratitude of the sufferer and moral
approval of those who know what he had done.

And yet, this will not always be the case. Suppose the
person in question is a lorry-driver who will be making this
very journey in any case: he simply wants company or someone to talk to him to keep him awake; he makes no change of
arrangements, of speed or route or time-table, for the sake
of the sick person; does the fact that his driving is the means
of bringing aid and comfort render his act morally good?
Presumably not; but then the good result is not his motive; it
is not his reason-for-acting; he does not act for the sake of it.

But given that the relief of suffering *is* his motive, his reason for acting, then some of its goodness is 'reflected' (in Bentham's phrase) on the act itself; that is, the act which it prompts is rendered worthy or commendable. The extent to which this is so will vary according as the good end was the agent's total or partial motive: as witness the modest person who seeks to belittle the merit of his deed by such self-depreciatory remarks as, 'I had to give the car a run some time to charge the battery', appealing implicitly to the premiss that, if the happy outcome of an act is not one's sole reason for doing it, one is correspondingly less to be commended for having done it. This is one qualification, then: whether or not, and the extent to which, one 'would have done it in any case'. There is another: whether or not the beneficent outcome was the sole consequence intended, or at least foreseen; as witness the modest person who says, 'I *enjoy* driving', or 'I had time on my hands; it was a relief to be doing something', or even, 'It's all good publicity for my business'. Of course, if the latter were his *sole* or total motive, e.g. if in fact he would not have made the drive if there were no publicity likely, the morally good consequence of the act does not render it morally good itself; but the fact that he believed that some such reward was likely, and hoped that it would ensue, does not strip his action of moral goodness if he would have performed it *in any case*. If the relief of the sufferer was his only motive, then the moral value of the act would be correspondingly higher. The act in question is a means to doing something morally good; therefore, in so far as a person intends to perform that act for the sake of that end, he intends to do what is morally good.

In many of these cases it is not only the act's moral value which is affected by the end for which it is performed; its characterization also may be altered: for morally indifferent acts are usually denoted by terms which we called in Chapter 1 'elidable'. The term which functions as a motive-term, given one description of the act, may come to function as the act-term, given another description of the performance. This is most commonly the case when an indifferent act is performed for the sake of a wrongful end; we shall often be less inclined to say that the motive vitiates the act than to describe the performance with a single, dyslogistic, act-term.

(ii) *Effect on good acts*

Next, what is the effect of motive on the morality of an act which is, of itself, good? In *Major Barbara*, Undershaft's wife remarks that he is always giving disreputable reasons for his most generous deeds; she obviously assumes that, if these protestations were true, his deeds would be deprived of their moral value. Indeed, Eliot's Becket declares that to yield to the temptations of sensuality, ambition, and treason would be less grievous than to yield to the fourth: 'The last temptation is the greatest treason, To do the right deed for the wrong reason.'

It seems clear at least that when the total motive for an act, whose object is of itself morally good, is an end which is evil, the act is deprived of all moral goodness and the whole performance is condemned as bad. To offer a meal to a hungry man is an act which is, of itself, morally good; but if one's sole motive is to induce him to commit a crime—say, making this a condition—one's act is vitiated. In such a case the act is performed simply and exclusively as a means to doing evil, and in no way for the sake of the goodness normally attached to it. The agent would perform the act with equal enthusiasm if it were morally neutral, or even immoral; he is simply not interested in the goodness of the act itself, but solely in its efficacy as a means to something which is bad. This recalls what was said in Chapter 3 about the absence of intentionality and consciousness as a disentitling circumstance; for an act to be judged morally good it is indeed a necessary condition that the act itself be good or at least permissible, but it is not sufficient: the agent must to some extent recognize and seek it as such. A rough parallel may be drawn with some aesthetic matters: if a person buys a Chippendale writing-table of rare beauty, his action suggests that he is a person of taste; but if it transpires that he wants it only for firewood, he stands revealed as a Philistine, and his action, which on the face of it argued some aesthetic feeling, is shown to be far removed from any such quality.

But what if the bad end is only a man's partial motive; if he hopes, indeed, to attain it, but also wants the good naturally associated with the act? A man gives an alms to a poor girl, partly indeed in the hope that she may give herself to him, but also in part because he is genuinely sorry for her: even if she refuses him, he has no intention of taking back the money. In such cases, is the act deprived of all moral value? I should think that it is not; for the agent satisfies the two conditions, each necessary but together sufficient, for a morally good act: viz. that the act itself is a good one, and that the agent to some extent recognizes and seeks it as such. Here the natural outcome of the act—i.e. the relief of poverty or suffering—is not seen and used solely as a means, an instrument, but partly at least for its own sake. It was suggested above that it is inappropriate to call Q the motive for the action X if Q is the natural accompaniment or outcome of X; properly speaking, every motive is in some sense 'ulterior' to the natural associate of the action it prompts; Q therefore may be credited with a moral value of its own, regardless of the end to which it is also directed, unless the agent repudiates that value and uses Q exclusively as an instrument in some immoral work. Where, then, the morally bad end is only partly the agent's motive for doing a deed which is of itself commendable, the deed itself does not seem to be deprived of moral value, and one does not say that the whole performance is bad *sans phrase*.

So far we have been considering good deeds prompted

by morally bad motives; but there is also an allied, though different, type: where the motive in question is not quite bad, but seems to be *unworthy*. A recent advertisement has been urging the employer to buy lunch-vouchers for his typist, because 'if she is properly fed at midday she will work better in the afternoon'. A nurse may be faithful and attentive to her patients, not only out of compassion for them or from a sense of duty, but in the hope of a good report from her ward-sister and hence quickened advancement. A politician is vigorous in fighting to have the Government create employment in distressed areas of his constituency, not only for the sake of relieving those out of work, but in the hope of ensuring his own re-election. Now such motives are not morally bad; it is not immoral to want one's employees to be efficient, or to seek advancement in one's profession or a seat in Parliament; but one feels that such motives are not worthy of the deeds they prompt, and fall short of what is called for. It is not that they are bad; but one feels that they are not good enough. I think that T. S. Eliot rather overlooks this distinction between the immoral motive and the unworthy one: in *Murder in the Cathedral*, the Fourth Tempter urges Becket to do what he believes to be right, for a number of motives which are very mixed indeed. Some are downright wicked, e.g. the pleasure of seeing his enemies eternally tormented in hell; but these are run together with some which are rather childish, or at any rate what I suggest calling 'unworthy', e.g. the pleasure of wielding the power of excommunication, and the prospect of his enemies' discomfiture after his martyrdom when they are forced to creep in penance to his shrine.

Now what is the bearing of an unworthy motive on our moral evaluation of the good deed that it prompts? Once again we must distinguish the cases of the total and the partial motive. Where the good deed is done, partly for its own sake and partly from an unworthy motive, there can be no question of condemning the agent's whole performance as base, for neither his act nor his motive is bad. But is it deprived of all moral value, reduced to some sort of blank neutrality? I should think that it is not; a real element of moral goodness seems to arise from the dual condition, first that the act is morally good, and second that this is to some extent sought for its own sake; no doubt the performance falls short of moral perfection to the extent that the unworthy motive prevails; but to the extent that the good object is what is pursued the performance seems to be good; no condition necessary for a good act seems to be missing. If this is not correct, the conclusion would be rather alarming: perfect disinterestedness is no doubt something very rare; but surely morally good actions are not all that rare. Few people would claim that their eye was single, their motives unmixedly pure. Such people would surely be rare, not only as near-saints, but also as extremely uncomplex characters: 'One deed, one motive' is not a rule taught us by experience. Perhaps one may again suggest a rough parallel in the field of aesthetics. A collector may well buy a treasure, partly out of genuine appreciation of its artistic merit, but stimulated too at the prospect of a rival's chagrin; one may rate his standing as a patron of the arts correspondingly a little lower, but one does not consider him devoid of taste or his choice unworthy of approval.

But what of the good deed done *solely* for the sake of an unworthy motive? The answer would seem to be different according as the good deed was or was not obligatory. In the case where it was obligatory, the agent seems to be in approximately the same case as a person who fails to perform an act he is obliged to do, and to approximately the same extent: for that the performance of an obligatory act should have moral value it seems necessary, not only that one go through the physical motions enjoined, but also that one do so as a moral agent: that is, in some sense perceiving the moral status of the action, and in some sense doing it for the sake of its moral goodness. In the case where the good deed was not obligatory, the fact that the agent's sole motive was an unworthy one seems to render his performance neither good nor bad. For instance, a person decides to become a blood-donor when payment is introduced; he has never given blood before, and the monetary inducement is his only reason for enrolling now; he makes it clear that, on any occasion when payment is not forthcoming, his services will not be available. One can hardly uphold his action as morally good, since the moral aspect simply does not enter into his considerations; the act is of itself good, but it is not for the sake of this goodness that he does it. On the other hand, one can hardly condemn his action as immoral, since he has neither done something wrong nor failed to do something obligatory.

There is a third type of motive that can prompt an action whose object is morally good: a motive which is morally good. This does not, of course, apply to the case where the agent's objective is the natural accompaniment or outcome of the action; such objectives, as we have seen, are not properly called motives at all: one does not say that a surgeon's *motive* for removing a growth is to cure the patient. But it is possible for a person both to perform the act in question for the sake of its natural outcome, and also for the sake of some further good end to which it may lead: a teacher may devote himself to teaching mathematics, not merely for the sake of his pupil's intellectual formation and to prepare him for a satisfying occupation when he leaves school, but also consciously seeking his country's betterment in the level of its scientific skill and achievement. Such good motives enhance the value of a performance, and may sometimes lead us to subsume the act under an additional moral species.

(iii) *Effect on bad acts*

Next, what is the effect of motive on the morality of an act which is, of itself, morally bad?

Where the motive also is a bad one, the question is quickly answered. There are two possibilities. One is that the act comes to fall within an additional species of wrongdoing. Aristotle's man who commits adultery for the sake of gain is guilty of injustice, not only of profligacy; the person who lies in order to betray his country is guilty of treason, not only of lying. The other possibility is that the wrongdoing is aggravated within a given species: as when a person assaults an enemy, not only to inflict pain on him, but also to disable him for life.

What if the act, of itself a bad one, is prompted by a good motive, i.e. if it is a means used for the sake of some good end? This much at least seems certain: that the presence of a worthy motive has *some* ameliorating effect on the perform-ance. Even the person who holds that a good end cannot justify the use of wicked means for its attainment will admit that it *mitigates* the agent's guilt. He may hold that to kill a person suffering from an incurable cancer in order to end his pain is still murder, and never permissible; but he will agree that it is less wicked than the same deed done for gain. But the question of the motive's *justifying* effect cannot be settled in the present essay, for one's answer to it depends on one's views about other ethical questions than those which fall within our scope. An extreme Utilitarian might say that the question cannot really be asked: if only the consequences at which the motive is directed are sufficiently happy, or suffi-ciently harm-preventing, then the act itself cannot be called a bad act; it is the whole train of events on which verdict should be passed, not some part of them in isolation from the rest. Some, as we have seen, would even re-describe the act in terms of its ultimate consequences. However, not every Utilitarian will reject the question; Bentham, for instance, writes:

Where an act is pernicious in its primary consequences the secondary mischief is not obliterated by the *goodness* of the motive;

though the motive be of the best kind. For, notwithstanding the goodness of the motive, an act of which the primary consequences are pernicious is produced by it in the instance in question, by the supposition.[1]

Most people will agree with this, as far as it goes; but some will take it further than others. Bentham himself holds that in some circumstances even to kill a man may be a beneficial act. It cannot very well be beneficial to the man himself; but if the total consequences of killing him were happier than the total consequences of not killing him, Bentham would consider the act of killing him justified, and even obligatory. Of course, it is open to a Utilitarian to attempt to show that the total consequences of killing an innocent man will always be worse than any other possible consequences and hence can never be justified. To pursue this would take us rather too far afield; for this question cannot be settled until one has settled the prior question, 'Are there any kinds of act which are always, in all circumstances, impermissible?' If the answer to that question is 'Yes', then it is wellnigh tautological to say that a good motive does not alter the morality of (such) bad acts. Still, even without straying from our own field, one or two things may be said.

From the thesis concerning non-elidable act-terms, put forward above in Chapter 1, we may derive a corollary: that there are some kinds of act which we know quite well how to characterize even before we know the agent's motive. Suppose that three different people each successfully procure the judicial condemnation and execution of an innocent man: one, in order to save five others threatened by lynch-law; one, in order to inherit the victim's fortune or office; one, for an undiscovered motive. Two things at least are clear. First, we can assign the appropriate species-term in each case, even the third: it is Judicial Murder. No matter what the motive of the third man transpired to be, the act will be

[1] p. 165.

described as an act of judicial murder if the definition of that term is fulfilled. Second, we can assign an appropriate genus-term: the act is an act of Injustice: indeed, Miss Anscombe has held that it is the paradigm case of Injustice. Now it was suggested above that genus-terms lend themselves more readily to serve as predicates than as subjects: they have less of the descriptive than of the evaluative about them. At least, then, one may say that the act is unjust, whatever the motive that prompted it. It remains that some philosophers would hold that in some circumstances such acts may be justified. This involves their saying that injustice is sometimes justified: that it is sometimes right to act unjustly. A man with the courage of his logic may grasp the nettle and say just that; but he appears to be committed to a further step: it seems that he must say that there are different rules for judging the same act when it is a means and when it is an end. There are many views as to what are the criteria for the moral evaluation of acts; but why should there be different criteria for evaluating an act, and the consequences of the act? Why should the same kind of act acquire some privileged status, some immunity from moral censure, when it is performed as a means, which it does not enjoy when it is an end? In each case the act is an intended human objective, and one might expect it to be judged according as it is or is not a worthy or proper or commendable objective of human activity or pursuit or experience. If there are reasons for saying that instances of a given moral species are bad, or wrong, one would expect that the unfavourable predicate applies to it whenever its definition was fulfilled, and hence that a person is equally disqualified from making it one's objective as an end or as a means. However, this is not the place to begin a discussion of the new group of problems which a pursuit of this question would involve: the problems of the identity, and rules of application, of the primary criteria for the moral evaluation of an act.

(iv) *Obliquely intentional consequences*

One last question. Suppose that a man performs an act for the sake of some worthy end, though realizing that some bad consequence will also follow: that is, he performs the act X knowing that the consequences P and Q will follow: to do or produce P is a good and commendable act, but to do or produce Q would normally be morally bad. In such circumstances, is he justified in doing X? The person who holds that an act is to be judged solely in terms of its consequences, and hence that any act is justified if its performance will produce, on balance, more good than will its omission, will not find the question particularly interesting; his answer is simply, 'Calculate'. But I suggest that a negative answer is not the only alternative: that even a person who holds that certain acts are never permissible may quite consistently hold that doing-X would be justified, given three conditions: (1) doing-X must not, of course, be one of the acts which he considers to be never permissible; (2) P and Q must be of comparable gravity, value, or importance; (3) Q must not be a means to obtaining or producing P, but simply a foreseen by-product of its production.

A critic of such a suggestion—Bentham, perhaps, for one—might, on general Utilitarian grounds, dismiss the first condition as pointless and accept the second as sufficient; but what of the third? We might borrow terminology from Bentham himself to express it: P must be directly intentional, but Q only obliquely so. He explains this distinction as follows:

A consequence may be said to be directly or lineally intentional, when the prospect of producing it constituted one of the links in the chain of causes by which the person was determined to do the act. It may be said to be obliquely or collaterally intentional when, although the consequence was in contemplation, and appeared likely to ensue in case of the act's being performed, yet the prospect of producing such consequence did not constitute a link in the aforesaid chain.[1]

This seems happier terminology than that of Peters, who would speak of Q as an *unintended consequence*.[2] He quotes the social scientist's finding that raising the level of education in a community also produces an increase in the suicide rate, the economist's theory that full employment also involves inflation, and the sociologist's claim that changes in the techniques of production bring with them characteristic changes in the social structure; he calls the secondary effect in each case an unintended consequence. Now if a person does X knowing that Q will be produced by it, one can hardly describe Q simply as 'unintended'; nor, if it is done solely for the sake of P, does one naturally describe it as 'intended'. As Hampshire and Hart have said, the man who shoots at someone knows, in a perfectly ordinary sense of 'know', that the act will involve the production of a loud noise; he therefore cannot be said to have made the noise unintentionally; and it would be misleading to say that he made it intentionally. It is useful, then, to have a term such as Bentham's 'obliquely intentional'. Such a term, incidentally, helps us to distinguish the present case from that considered earlier, where a man performed a morally indifferent act with two partial motives, one good and one bad. In that case both the foreseen consequences were directly intended; in the present case, the good one is directly intentional, the bad one only obliquely so.

Now although Bentham makes this distinction early in his Chapter 8, he nowhere invokes it as relevant to the moral or legal appraisal of an act. In this I think that he is quite consistent, for the distinction is irrelevant to the question of *control*. The production or non-production of the harmful consequences is within the agent's control as much as is the production or non-production of the good consequence.

[1] p. 84.   [2] 'Motives and Motivation', loc. cit., p. 127.

There is therefore no question of his being *excused* for the obliquely intentional production of the harmful consequence; and the question of his being *justified* turns, for Bentham, solely on the balance of good or ill that arises. But we are considering the question from the point of view of a person who requires more than that to justify a course of conduct: of a person who holds, for instance, that murder, defined as the intentional killing of an innocent man, is always wrong.

Let us compare two rather lurid cases, suggested by recent newspaper reports. First, a time-bomb is found by a group of people locked in an upstairs room. Their only means of escaping death is to throw the bomb out of the single window, and it is seen that it will land near a solitary man below who has no chance of escape. Second, a party of people pot-holing are trapped by an over-stout companion who is wedged inextricably in the hole which is their only way of escape, and their only access to air. With sincere reluctance they decide that, all other attempts having failed, their only hope of salvation is to remove the human obstacle with dynamite. In each of these two cases several lives may be saved at the expense of one. But there is a difference. In the second case the destruction of the one man is, in Bentham's phrase, directly intentional; if the dynamite fails to explode, or if it fails to destroy the human obstacle, the desired result will not be obtained, and another attempt must be made. In the former case, the killing of the man downstairs is only obliquely intentional; it is not a means necessary for obtaining the desired result, for if by some happy chance the bomb failed to explode, or the blast of its explosion did no harm to the man, the people upstairs would still be saved: 'although the consequence was in contemplation, and appeared likely to ensue in case of the act's being performed, yet the prospect of producing the consequence did not constitute a link in the aforesaid chain'. In the second case the victim's death is intended, albeit reluctantly and only as a means to a worthy end; in the first case it is not intended, though one cannot call it unintended: it is obliquely intentional. The person, then, who holds that murder is never justified, whether as an end or as a means, could therefore hold that the action taken in the first case was permissible while condemning that taken in the second.

I should think that one might put forward a similar explanation of one's passing different judgement on two cases which we have mentioned: killing babies in order to provide infant bodies for medical research, and raising the level of education in a community with a consequent increase in the suicide rate. In each case the (at least obvious) good and bad consequences bear comparison: the advancement of learning, and the death of a number of people. But common sense suggests that the second is quite justified and the first quite wicked. I think that we may offer a theoretical vindication of that common-sense judgement in terms of the distinction which we have been making. The deaths of the babies were directly intended, and the definition of murder was verified in them no less literally for their being designed as a means to a worthy enough end. But one would not describe the deaths of the suicides as 'intended' by the person who launches the new educational programme; they are not designed as a means to securing the advancement of learning, and should the suicides not occur the desired consequence will be obtained just as successfully. They in no wise verify the definition of murder; they are only obliquely intended. In the language of accountancy, they are a realized but unwanted cost.

Here we leave the question. To pursue it would involve vindicating, first, the definition of murder as the directly intended killing of an innocent person, and second, the contention that murder thus defined is never justified. That leads on to many other issues. People who agree wholeheartedly that the killing of the babies calls for the severest moral censure will be far from unanimous about the reasons that warrant such a verdict. Bentham remarks a little acidly that men are more prone to invoke such conclusions in support of their premisses than to derive the conclusions from the premisses. Hampshire has said that it seems impossible to investigate the general grounds upon which some human activities are to be preferred to others, and at the same time remain neutral between the different schools of moral theory; and at three or four points in the last few pages we have borne implicit witness to the justice of that remark.

INDEX

PRINTED IN GREAT BRITAIN
AT THE UNIVERSITY PRESS, OXFORD
BY VIVIAN RIDLER
PRINTER TO THE UNIVERSITY